Selected Titles in This Series

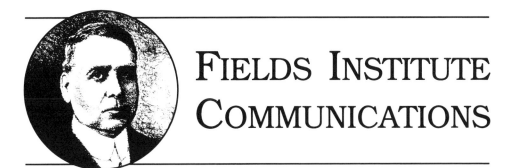

FIELDS INSTITUTE
COMMUNICATIONS

THE FIELDS INSTITUTE FOR RESEARCH IN MATHEMATICAL SCIENCES

Topology and Markets

Graciela Chichilnisky
Editor

American Mathematical Society
Providence, Rhode Island

The Fields Institute
for Research in Mathematical Sciences

The Fields Institute is named in honour of the Canadian mathematician John Charles Fields (1863–1932). Fields was a visionary who received many honours for his scientific work, including election to the Royal Society of Canada in 1909 and to the Royal Society of London in 1913. Among other accomplishments in the service of the international mathematics community, Fields was responsible for establishing the world's most prestigious prize for mathematics research—the Fields Medal.

The Fields Institute for Research in Mathematical Sciences is supported by grants from the Ontario Ministry of Education and Training and the Natural Sciences and Engineering Research Council of Canada. The Institute is sponsored by McMaster University, the University of Toronto, the University of Waterloo, and York University and has affiliated universities in Ontario and across Canada.

1991 *Mathematics Subject Classification.* Primary 00A69, 57N65, 57Rxx, 62Cxx, 90D35, 90A60, 90A80, 90Axx, 90Dxx.

Library of Congress Cataloging-in-Publication Data
Chichilnisky, Graciela.
    Topology and markets / Graciela Chichilnisky.
        p. cm. — (Fields Institute Communications, ISSN 1069-5265 ; 22)
    Includes bibliographical references (p.   ).
    ISBN 0-8218-1071-5 (alk. paper)
    1. Economics—Mathematical models—Congresses. 2. Capital market—Mathematical models—Congresses. I. Title. II. Series.
HB135.C475 1998
330′.01′5118—dc21
                                                98-44414
                                               CIP

Contents

Preface

Mathematics is an evolving language. Its evolution is driven by insights that lead to new fields of mathematical research. For a long time mathematics has emerged from a desire to understand the physical world. In trying to understand the universe to which we belong, Poincaré, in the last century, created the fields of topology and dynamical systems to explain celestial mechanics.

Great mathematics is the confluence of great topics of applications and the rigorous formalization that allows us to codify knowledge, create new structures and find unexpected connections. The power of mathematics is measured by the distance between what is assumed and what is proved; the creative tension is the distance between rigor and formalization, and the intuition needed for opening new frontiers.

Today we face a new scientific frontier, at the edge of social evolution and the impact that humans have on nature. This frontier leads to new mathematical questions and research. It includes economic issues about how humans organize themselves and distribute resources, their impact on nature, and the tension between individual goals and social goals. Markets emerge in this context as a powerful instrument of social organization and resource allocation. To explore this new frontier a workshop on *Geometry, Topology and Markets* took place from July 23 to 28 of 1994 at The Fields Institute for Research in Mathematical Sciences in Waterloo, Ontario. The participants came from far apart and had very diverse backgrounds, but they wished to communicate and advance a new field that involves topology and dynamical systems for the understanding of developments in the organization of markets. The workshop allowed the presentation and discussion of original mathematical results leading to applications in the economics of markets.[1]

The title of the workshop reflects the use of *qualitative* mathematics applied to the theory of markets. Qualitative, structural results are useful in the social sciences, such as economics, where measurements are often unreliable. Indeed the beginnings of the mathematical theory of markets was closely connected with topology: John Von Neumann, who formalized and produced one of the first proofs of existence of a market equilibrium, remarked that his result depended on topological tools such as fixed point theorems, and that there was no other way to obtain such results than by using topological tools. Market equilibrium, as represented in most articles in this book, can be understood as the solutions to a system of simultaneous non-linear equations. Finding such solutions requires typically topological tools.

Despite the natural role of topology in economics, during the last fifty years mathematical economics has been dominated by calculus, and particularly convex

---

[1] A copy of the program follows.

calculus. Our Workshop revisited this issue, focussing on geometrical and topological tools. The articles included in this volume belong to a classical approach to economics. They return to those mathematical tools and fields, topology and dynamical systems, that made the theory of markets amenable to mathematical analysis in the first place.

This book presents a cross-section of the topics covered in the Workshop. The first three days were devoted to mini-courses in mathematics aimed at providing the background, and the remaining time allowed the presentation of new theorems, along with their applications to the theory of markets. We discussed new topological invariants for the existence and the characterization of market equilibria and their relation with social choice and to other forms of resource allocation such as game theory, to competitive and cooperative systems, algebraic topology and geometry and social choice, computational complexity and stochastic processes in financial markets.

In the first paper, Morris Hirsch studies applications of dynamical systems to deterministic and stochastic economic models. This article gives a remarkably simple survey of main concepts in dynamical systems and provides a large number of results linking economic models of different types. Hirsch is concerned with modelling economies in which production becomes more efficient when the scale increases, namely economies with *increasing returns to scale*. Beyond a certain point, however, the returns decrease thus ensuring that the system as a whole lives in a compact domain. Hirsch asks how the states of the system evolve through time. His point of view is to focus on whether a given class of systems is convergent, every trajectory tending to an equilibrium or fixed point. This point of view is emphasized throughout, although oscillatory and chaotic systems are considered briefly in Section 10. More elaborated market models are introduced in Section 5, recent dynamical theory in Section 6, and this is applied to Bertrand competition in the following section. In the last three sections Hirsch explores stochastic dynamical systems. In Section 9 he looks at allocation processes, which are generalized Polya urn processes, in which the limiting behavior of such a process corresponds to a vector field associated to the process. In Section 11 he turns to another mathematical subject: game theory, treating games that are played repeatedly by the same players (he considers only two players) whose payoff matrices are subject to random perturbations. Players adopt long term policies leading to a description of the evolution of their strategies as stochastic processes that are very similar to urn models. As with much of Hirsch's work, this paper will be valuable in a number of disciplines for years to come.

The second paper achieves also a somewhat surprising result: a unification of four different concepts in the economics of resource allocation, that were previously considered distinct: financial arbitrage, market equilibrium, the core and social choice. This article shows that the key to this unification is a new *topological invariant*, which is defined from the preferences and the endowments of the traders of a Walrasian economy. This is based on the cohomology ring of the *nerve* of a family of cones, each cone corresponding to a trader and representing the traders that improve its utility. From this topological invariant one defines limited arbitrage, and shows that it is simultaneously necessary and sufficient for the existence of a competitive equilibrium, the nonemptiness of the core and for the existence of social choice rules as defined above. When limited arbitrage does not hold, *social diversity* of various degrees is defined by the properties of the topological invariant. The tenet of this article is that a topological object, the invariant CH, serves to define a concept that has been elusive until recently, social diversity, and to show that while a certain amount of diversity is useful to ensure gains from trade, beyond a certain point diversity does not allow the functioning of the most frequently used forms of resource allocation, by games markets and social choice. Another way of looking at the same issue is that current economic institutions function only with relatively homogeneous societies, and if diversity is desired for the resilience of the human species, we may have to develop new forms of resource allocation. This piece is idiosyncratic in its topic and the techniques that it utilizes, and proposes a unified way of understanding resource allocation in economics.

The following article, by Mark Broadie and Jérôme Detemple, is an excellent presentation of the state of the art in financial mathematics, involving the pricing of American Options on assets that pay dividends, such as corporate stocks. American options differ from European options in that they can be exercised at any time at or before maturity date. Instead, European options can only be exercised at the fixed maturity date. Broadie and Detemple develop a model where the price of one stock follows a stochastic differential equation involving the dividend rate on the stock, and the drift and volatility coefficients of the stocks' total rate of return. These three coefficients are bounded and progressively measurable processes of the filtration which defines the flow of information in the economy. Beginning with a review of the valuation principles for European options, they extend the analysis to American options and present the early exercise premium and the delayed exercise premium representations of the American option price. They specialize the results to a standard model when the underlying asset price follows a geometric Brownian motion process and the interest rate is constant. They also consider American capped options with constant and growing caps. They present here previously unpublished results for capped options on non-dividend paying assets when the underlying asset price follows an Ito process with stochastic volatility and the caps' growth is an adapted stochastic process. Of all the articles, this one is the closest to Hirsch's in incorporating formally the stochastic nature of the economy.

The fourth and final article starts from two axioms that capture the idea of sustainable development. The axioms require that neither the present nor the future should play a dictatorial role. From these axioms emerged a representation theorem yielding a distinctive welfare criterion and a new form of cost benefit analysis. The current article asks whether the earlier results can be extended to ensure equal treatment not just for the present and the future, but also for other groups through time. The answer is negative. However, by limiting the diversity of the groups (to linearly ordered ultrafilters), the results can be recovered.

The Fields Workshop was an intellectually stimulating, lively and enjoyable event, and I am pleased to offer to the reader some of the pieces that were presented and discussed. These pieces point out the mathematics needed to understand markets, and the connections between contemporary tools of topology and dynamical systems for the analysis of classic issues on economics: financial arbitrage, markets, games and social choice.

Graciela Chichilnisky
Editor

January 1998

THE FIELDS INSTITUTE FOR RESEARCH IN MATHEMATICAL SCIENCES

Workshop on
Geometry, Topology and Markets

Saturday, July 23 to Thursday, July 28, 1994
The Fields Institute, Waterloo, Ontario, Canada

Workshop Follow-up
July 29, 1994
Columbia University, New York, New York, U. S. A.

Recent developments have deepened the connection between topology and the economics of markets. This workshop will allow the presentation and discussion of original mathematical results, which have or could lead to useful applications in the economics of markets. The first three days of the workshop will be devoted to a series of mini-courses in mathematics aimed at providing the basic background. The remaining time will allow the presentation of new theorems, along with their applications to the theory of markets. Topics discussed will include: new topological invariants for existence, characterization and computation of market equilibria and their relation to social choice and to other forms of resource allocation, competitive and cooperative systems, algebraic geometry and markets with increasing returns, computational complexity, and stochastic processes and financial markets.

Organizing committee

G. Chichilnisky, Chair, Organizing Committee
(Columbia University-Stanford University)
S. Cappell (New York University)
J. Detemple (McGill University)
M. Hirsch (University of California, Berkeley)
A. Khan (The Johns Hopkins University)
M. Shub (Thomas J. Watson Research Center, IBM)

Mini-Course Program
July 23 to July 25, 1994

Lattice Points and Polytopes	S. Cappell
Topology & Markets	G. Chichilnisky
Dynamical Systems and Economic Models	M. Hirsch

Invited Speakers

R. Abraham	University of California, Santa Cruz
Y. Baryshnikov	University of Osnabrück, Germany
V. Böhm	University of Mannheim, Germany
J. C. Candeal	University of Zaragoza, Spain
J. Detemple	McGill University
E. Dierker	University of Vienna
D. Foley	Barnard College, Columbia University
I. Gluzyrina	Chite Institute of Natural Resources, Russia
G. Heal	Columbia Business School
E. Indurain-Eraso	Universidad Publica de Navarra, Spain
A. Kahn	The Johns Hopkins University
G. Koshevoy	Central Economics & Mathematics Institute, Russia
L. Lauwers	ETEW, Belgium
G. Saari	Northwestern University
W. Shafer	University of Illinois, Urbana-Champaign
L. S. Shapley	University of California, Los Angeles
M. Shub	Thomas J. Watson Research Center, IBM
Y. Sun	National University of Singapore
W. Truckel	Bielefeld University, Germany
N. Yannelis	University of Illinois, Urbana-Champaign

Co-Sponsored by the Columbia Business School and the U. S. National Science Foundation.

Supported by the Ontario Ministry of Education and Training and the Natural Sciences and Engineering Research Council of Canada.

Fields Institute Communications
Volume **22**, 1999

Applications of Dynamical Systems to Deterministic and Stochastic Economic Models

Morris W. Hirsch
Department of Mathematics
University of California at Berkeley
Berkeley, CA 94720-3840, USA
`hirsch@math.berkeley.edu`

Abstract. Markets and related games are modeled by several types of deterministic and stochastic dynamical systems. In simple cases, long run behavior of all or most trajectories can be determined. Convergence to stable equilibria is emphasized. After reviewing dynamical systems concepts, applications are made to X. Vives' oligopoly games, including Bertrand competition in differentiated markets. Limiting behavior of a class of stochastic processes is shown to be closely related to deterministic dynamical systems. These results are applied to B. Arthur's urn models of stochastic allocation processes, and to repeated games in which players use the long term strategy of fictitious play.

1 Introduction

Dynamical systems theory provides a mathematical way of looking at *processes* of all kinds where long-term behavior is of importance — biological, chemical, physical, etc. Many economic processes have been modeled as mathematical dynamical systems; (see, for example [**30**], [**10**]).

There is a peculiarity in economic systems, especially markets, that makes it difficult to model them as dynamical systems: The essence of an economy is *choice*, while the motivating idea of dynamical systems is *determinism*. One way of seeing this problem is to first look at how mathematics deals with somewhat analogous problems in physics and biology. The mathematics of Newtonian mechanics has no difficulty in writing down differential equations of motion for any number of perfectly elastic particles. In principle, then, such equations describe a perfect, ideal gas. But we are then helpless to derive any conclusions from this enormous set of equations. In any case, we are not interested in following the detailed trajectories of these particles. What we want is some useable description of the *ensemble* behavior, in terms of a small number of measurable quantities.

1991 *Mathematics Subject Classification.* 00A69, 90D35, 90Dxx, 57Rxx.
Partially supported by a grant from the National Science Foundation.

This is exactly what statistical mechanics does — in terms of temperature, entropy and pressure. These are properties of the ensemble which are not easily expressible in terms of the variables — position, momentum, acceleration — describing states of individual particles.

The problem in fluid mechanics is much worse — we don't even have language to describe the large-scale behavior of a turbulent fluid, and the relevant partial differential equations are difficult to analyze; even the existence of solutions is problematical.

In these examples the problem lies with the complexity of a system made up of a very large number of well-understood particles. Turning to biology, we find a further problem: each individual "particle" — nerve cell, organism, species — is extremely complex. And while physics has laws, such as conservation of energy and the second law of thermodynamics, which give quantitative restrictions on ensemble behavior, analogous laws in biology have yet to be discovered. In market economics the "particles" are individual economic agents. Here we face both the problem of large scale aggregation of individual activities, as well as the problem of choice, absent in physics.

In modeling large scale ensembles it seems necessary to assume that quantities describing activities of individuals can somehow be lumped or averaged so as to yield a set of numbers sufficient to describe (for modeling purposes) the instantaneous state of ensemble behavior.[1]

Once we have settled on such quantities, the next task is to discover the laws describing how the state changes with time. These laws constitute the *dynamic* of the system. Two common modeling methodologies are to postulate (1) deterministic dynamics, or (2) stochastic dynamics.

In the deterministic market models investigated here, we assume that each agent acts in a way which (she thinks) will maximize, or at least increase, her immediate profit, or rate of profit.

In the stochastic game models, we assume agents' actions can be described in probabilistic terms, even though each agent may be acting deterministically in the light of her knowledge. This knowledge, however, may depend on exogenous "random" quantities. This is not the same as postulating that each agent makes a random choice — whatever that may mean. Rather this approach assumes that the distribution of choices over an ensemble of similar agents behaves according to probabilistic laws.

In many writings on economic theory, a third procedure is used for resolving the choice-determinism dilemma: Ignore it, and simply assume that a kind of state defined as an "equilibrium" is reached — without specifying any dynamical system for which it is an equilibrium! While such approach may be useful, it will not be pursued here.

Given the description of the conceivable states of the system, and the dynamic (or the stochastic), the mathematician's task is *to derive laws describing how states of the system evolve in time*. While this problem can be stated as a question in pure mathematics, in reality our intuitions and insights into the original problem are crucial here. We may hope for useful dialog between mathematicians familiar with the relevant branches of dynamical systems, and scientists trying to model a natural system.

---

[1] The celebrated impossibility theorems of Arrow, and Chichilnisky, illustrate the the difficulty of agglomerating individual choices in plausible ways.

While very simple equations can specify extremely complex dynamical systems, one of the most important uses of dynamical theory has been to determine condition enabling us to decide whether a given class of systems is *convergent* — every trajectory tending to an equilibrium (fixed point). This point of view is emphasized throughout, although oscillatory and chaotic systems are considered briefly in Section 11.[2]

After looking at a very simple dynamical model of duopoly in Section 2 as an introduction to dynamical ideas, we review basic dynamical concepts in the next three sections. These are applied to a more elaborate market model in Section 6. Some recent dynamical theory is presented in the next section, and applied to Bertrand competition in the following section.

In the final three sections we look at a very different class of models; rather than being deterministic, they are stochastic. Yet these particular models — generalized Polya urns and repeated games with uncertainty — are of such a nature that in the long run their behavior is closely connected with deterministic systems of differential equations — a kind of dynamical analog to the law of large numbers. Therefore knowledge of the dynamics of the differential equation leads to knowledge of the limiting behavior of sample paths of the stochastic process. This has long been known for very simple vector fields; recent new results of this kind are presented here.

In Section 10 we look at stochastic allocation processes, which have been used to model competing technologies. There is a precise sense in which the limiting behavior of such a process corresponds to limiting behavior of a vector field associated to the process.

The allocation processes we consider are just the same as generalized Polya urn processes. In Section 11 further dynamic results are applied to these processes. Under certain conditions we conclude that almost surely a sample path tracks a trajectory of the vector field. This leads to the construction of oscillatory and even chaotic urn models.

In Section 12 we turn to another mathematical subject that has been used for economic models, and in fact was inspired by economics, namely Game Theory. Here we treat games played repeatedly by the same players (for simplicity we consider two players), whose payoff matrices are subject to random perturbations, where players adopt long-term policies leading to a description of the evolution of their strategies as stochastic processes very similar to urn models. Again a dynamical system aids in the analysis of long-term behavior.

2 A simple model

We consider a simple example of the oligopoly games treated by X. Vives [29], of the type he calls "Cournot competition in differentiated markets".

Consider two competing producer-sellers, $\mathcal{A}_1$ and $\mathcal{A}_2$, of the same commodity. Each decides independently what quantity $x_i\,(i = 1, 2)$ to produce; we assume it will all be sold. The market arrives at a unit price[3] p, which is a function $p = p(x_1 + x_2)$. Producer $\mathcal{A}_i$ makes profit

$$\Pi_i = x_i(p - C_i)$$

---

[2]At present the rigorous mathematical theory of chaotic dynamical systems is very undeveloped. The most useful service it has thus far performed for science is simply to demonstrate beyond doubt that chaotic systems are prevalent — and that most of them are impossible to analyze rigorously, or even describe crudely. We lack not only theorems, but language.

[3]Vives deals with inverse demand instead of price.

where $C_i = C_i(x_i)$ is her total unit cost. Each agent then revises her production goal.

How should we model this?

The first modeling issue is to describe the *set of conceivable states of the system*. We assume provisionally that the production level x_i can be any nonnegative real number; more realistically we could restrict production levels to some finite interval. We take the state of the system at any time to be a vector $x = (x_1, x_2)$. The *state space* is therefore the space $\mathbf{R}^2_+$ of ordered pairs of nonnegative real numbers.

We also postulate that the price p is a nonnegative function of production.

The next question is: What kind of *time* are we using? In a *discrete time* model all quantities are recalculated at a succession of equal time intervals, usually days or years. In a *continuous time* model, we imagine continuously changing quantities, governed by a differential equation. Both choices have advantages and disadvantages, and in many situations neither is particulary realistic (imagine transactions taking place at random times). But we are not trying to describe reality, only to model it. For a discrete time model, the time variable t takes values in the $\mathbf{Z}$ of integers or in the set $\mathbf{N} = \{0, 1, 2, \dots\}$ of natural numbers. For a continuous time model, t lies in the set $\mathbf{R}$ or real numbers, or in the set $\mathbf{R}_+$ of nonnegative real numbers.

Now the crucial question: how do states evolve as time passes? Suppose we consider a discrete time system, taking $t \in \mathbf{N}$. Given the state $x(t)$ at time t, what can we say about the state $x(t+1)$?

To answer this we must make some assumptions about the producers' behaviors. We assume here that each wants to increase profit. Here the problem of choice versus determinism is evident: There may be many ways to increase profit.

A standard way to proceed is to specify a range of choice for each producer, depending on current production levels and price, and then to analyze all the possible sequences of events that may ensue. The resulting mathematical formalism is not generally thought of as a dynamical system, and the standard results of dynamical system theory do not apply.

To obtain a deterministic dynamical system we need some assumption that completely determines a producer's behavior in terms of the *current* prices, costs and production levels. A simple (to state!), classical assumption is:

> *Each producer acts to maximize profit assuming that the production*
> *level of the other producer is unchanged.*

Thus $x_i(t+1) = y_i$, where y_i maximizes

$$y_i(p(y_i + x_j(t)) - C_i(y_i))$$

for $i, j \in \{1, 2\}, i \neq j$. Implicit in this formulation is the unrealistic assumption that *each producer has complete knowledge of the price function p*. More on this later.

The system is not yet deterministic: We need to assume that such y_i are unique. This can be guaranteed by various assumptions, but here we don't need to specify them. Thus we simply assume:

> *For each i and each $\xi \in \mathbf{R}$, the function*
>
> $$\eta \to \eta(p(\eta + \xi) - C_i(\eta))$$
>
> *takes its maximum value at a unique $\eta = f_i(\xi) \in [0, \infty)$.*

Under this uniqueness assumption, we see that the production vector $x(t + 1)$ depends only on $x(t)$. Thus there is a map

$$F : \mathbf{R}_+^2 \to \mathbf{R}_+^2 \qquad (2.1)$$

such that $x(t + 1) = F(x(t))$.

This map is the dynamic of our system. Starting from any initial state $a \in \mathbf{R}_+^2$, we obtain a sequence of production vectors $a = a_0, a_1, \ldots$ where $a_{n+1} = F(a_n)$ for $n \in \mathbf{N}$. This sequence is the *trajectory* of the initial state a. We also write this as $a_n = F^n(a)$, where F^n denotes the n'th iterate of F, that is, the composition $F \circ \cdots \circ F$ of F with itself n times (and F^0 denotes the identity map).

Notice that F has the special form

$$F(x_1, x_2) = (f_1(x_2), f_2(x_1)) \qquad (2.2)$$

where f_i solves the maximization problem described above.

The main dynamic question is: *What happens in the long run?* To attack this problem we need to know the nature of the map F, which in turn depends on the price function p and the unit cost functions C_i.

It is natural (and almost unavoidable) to postulate that the exogenous function $p : \mathbf{R}_+ \to \mathbf{R}_+$ is nonincreasing. To simplify matters we assume also that p is continuously differentiable with negative derivative.

What is to prevent our agents from raising production levels past all bounds? Recall that we assumed the market absorbed all production; this is unreasonable if we allow unlimited production. So we need to postulate some feature of our model which prevents unlimited production.

A natural way to do this is to assume that at high production levels, unit costs exceed prices and both profit levels Π_i are negative. Since we are also assuming prices decrease with total production, we postulate:

There exists $z_* > 0$ such that if $z \geq z_*$ then $p(z) < C_i(z)$, $i = 1, 2$.

We of course assume both producers know of such a z_*. This ensures that each producer will always keep her production level below z_*.

With this assumption we can effectively limit the state space to $[0, z_*] \times [0, z_*]$; this space, being compact, has great technical advantages. More precisely, the system is dissipative (Section 3), attracted to a subset of $[0, z_*] \times [0, z_*]$.

It is reasonable to assume that production is feasible, i.e., profitable for each producer, at *some* production levels — otherwise one or both producers would go out of business.

We want to use calculus if possible, so we want all our functions to be continuously differentiable (denoted by C^1). While to assume p and C_i are C^1 seems innocuous, it is not reasonable to assume that F is C^1, since we have already prescribed a complicated derivation of F from p and the C_i. We had better try to find some plausible additional assumption which implies F is C^1.

We consider f_1 in detail, the case of f_2 being similar. By definition, $f_1(\xi)$ is that value of η (assumed unique) where the function $\eta \mapsto \eta(p(\eta + \xi) - C_i(\eta))$ takes its maximum value. Define

$$G(\xi, \eta) = \eta(p(\eta + \xi) - C_i(\eta)).$$

Then $f_1(\xi)$ satisfies

$$\frac{\partial G}{\partial \eta}(\xi, f_1(\xi)) = 0.$$

Now $\partial G/\partial \eta$ is the function

$$J(\xi,\eta) = \eta p'(\xi+\eta) + p(\xi+\eta) - C_1'(\eta).$$

Thus $f_1(\xi)$ is locally defined implicitly as the solution to the equation

$$J(\xi, f_1(\xi)) = 0.$$

The implicit function theorem says that f_1 is C^1 provided that

$$\frac{\partial J(\xi,\eta)}{\partial \eta} \neq 0$$

wherever $J(\xi,\eta) = 0$, and in this case

$$f_1'(\xi) = -\frac{J_\xi(\xi, f_1(\xi))}{J_\eta(\xi, f_1(\xi))}$$

where J_η denotes $\partial J/\partial \eta$, etc.

Now

$$\frac{\partial J(\xi,\eta)}{\partial \eta} = \eta p''(\xi+\eta) + 2p'(\xi+\eta) - C_1''(\eta).$$

Some thought shows that as we have already assumed $p' < 0$, the only reasonable way to guarantee this is different from zero (taking $\eta = f_1(\xi)$) is to postulate that each summand is ≤ 0. There is nothing for it but to make the new assumptions:

$$p'' \leq 0, \quad C_i'' \leq 0.$$

And of course we are now assuming C_i and p are C^2 (continuous second partials).

Are these assumptions plausible? $C_i'' \leq 0$ is easily obtained by the drastic but common assumption of *linear* cost functions: $C_i(x_i) = \alpha x_i + \beta_i$. More generally it can be interpreted as requiring that marginal costs $C_i'(x_i)$ decrease (or don't increase) with increased production. At least this is economically meaningful, and not absurd.

The assumption of a concave price function $p(s)$ (i.e., $p'' \leq 0$) seems less natural to me, but I leave it to economists to justify or discard it.

The assumption of concave pricing has an important mathematical implication, namely that $f_i' < 0$. For by the implicit function theorem we have (suppressing arguments of functions):

$$f_1' = -\frac{J_\xi}{J_\eta};$$

we already know that $J_\eta < 0$, and one easily sees that

$$J_\xi = \eta p'' + p' < 0,$$

proving that $f_1' < 0$; and the proof for f_2 is similar.

This leads to an interesting conclusion about the long-term dynamical behavior of the system:

Theorem 2.1 *Every trajectory of the system approaches an orbit of period 2 (possibly a fixed point).*

This means that for any initial state a there is a state b with the following properties:

1. b has *period 2*, meaning that $F^2(b) := F(F(b)) = b$;
2. the distance from $F^n(a)$ to the orbit of b (the set consisting of b and $F(b)$) goes to zero.

Proof   Recalling the formula (2.2) for F, we see that the second iterate F^2 is defined by the formula

$$F^2(x_1, x_2) = (g_1(x_1), g_2(x_2))$$

where

$$g_1 = f_1 \circ f_2, \; g_2 = f_2 \circ f_1.$$

Then

$$g_1'(z) = f_1'(f_2(z))f_2'(z)) > 0$$

and similarly for g_2'. This shows that g_i is strictly increasing; therefore for any initial state (a_1, a_2), the limit $b_i = \lim_{n\to\infty}(g_i)^n(a_i)$ exists. The resulting state (b_1, b_2) has the required properties.   □

I return to this example in Section 9. Before leaving it, however, consider how technical mathematical considerations, such as differentiability, have led us to postulate economically meaningful properties of markets, such as concavity of cost and price functions. This illustrates an important but little-understood influence of mathematics in science.

3 Dynamical systems

A dynamical system comprises a set X called the *state space* together with a rule called the *dynamic* for how states evolve in time. Here the state space is taken to be Euclidean n-space $\mathbf{R}^n$ comprising all n-tuples real numbers, or more generally a subset such as an orthant or n-cube. Each state vector $x \in \mathbf{R}^n$ is thought of as a numerical coding for a conceivable[4] state of the economic system of interest. The dynamic is a collection Φ of maps $\Phi_t : X \to X$, indexed by real numbers t. For convenience we may also write $\Phi_t(x) = \Phi(t, x)$.

For any state $x \in X$ and $t > 0$ we interpret $\Phi_t(x)$ as the state to which x evolves after t units of time have elapsed; and, if negative times are allowed, for $-t < 0$ we think of $\Phi_{-t}(x)$ as the state which evolved into x from t units of time in the past. The map Φ_0 always denotes the identity map of X.[5]

The index t runs either through the set $\mathbf{R}_+$ of nonnegative real numbers — "continuous time" — or the set $\mathbf{N} = \{0, 1, 2 \ldots\}$ of natural numbers — "discrete time". Negative time usually has no practical meaning, but it often makes sense mathematically and can be theoretically useful. When negative times are allowed we always assume the maps Φ_t are one-to-one. Such a systems is called *reversible*. In this case the maps Φ_t and Φ_{-t} are inverse to each other.

The dynamic for a continuous time system is usually specified implicitly by a differential equation of the form $dy/dt = F(t, y), y(0) = x$, and defining $\Phi_t(x) = y(t)$.[6]

The theory of dynamical systems is most highly developed for *autonomous systems*, for which the dynamic obeys the *composition law* $\Phi_t \circ \Phi_s = \Phi_{t+s}$. Here the composition $x \mapsto g(f(x))$ of maps g, f is denoted by $g \circ f$. For a reversible

---

[4]Not necessarily a *possible* state! A dynamical systems model of a real system is nothing more than an elaborate thought-experiment.

[5]To be precise, some of the maps Φ_t may be defined only on a proper subset of X, as for example in the dynamics of the differential equation in one variable $dx/dt = x^2$. In almost all applications it is assumed, or provable without inordinate labor, that trajectories are defined at least for all $t \geq 0$.

[6]Here it is necessary to assume that the function $F(t, x)$ is continuously differentiable, or more generally, continuous in (t, x) and *locally Lipschitz* in x. Such assumptions validate the standard theorems on existence, uniqueness and continuity of solutions to the differential equations.

autonomous system it is easy to see that the maps Φ_t and Φ_{-t} are inverse to each other, so that in this case each Φ_t is a homeomorphism.

The dynamic for a discrete time autonomous system is given by a map g from the state space X to itself; we set $\Phi_k(x) = g^k(x)$ where g^k denotes the composition of g with itself k times (and g^0 denotes the identity map of X).

A continuous-time system is autonomous if it is defined by an autonomous (vector) differential equation, that is, an equation of the form $dx/dt = F(x)$, in which the right-hand side does not explicitly involve t.[7] For such a system the collection of maps $\{\Phi_t\}$ is called the *solution flow* of the differential equations. We can rarely get an explicit formula for these maps, but many properties of the family of all solutions can be described in terms of them.

All systems are henceforth assumed to be autonomous unless the contrary is stated. The dynamic is assumed to be given by a smooth vector field (for continuous-time systems) or a smooth mapping (for discrete-time systems) unless the contrary is stated.

3.1 Orbits, limit sets, equilibria and cycles. Consider now an autonomous dynamical system (X, Φ), for either discrete or continuous time. The *trajectory* of a point $x \in X$ is the mapping $t \mapsto \Phi_t(x)$. For a discrete-time systems this is a possibly infinite sequence of points of X; for a continuous-time system, a parameterized curve in X. For a differential equation the trajectory of a state is the solution that passes through the state at time 0.

The image of the trajectory of state x is a subset of X called the *orbit* of x. The orbit comprises all states to which x can evolve in the future, and (for reversible systems), from which x has evolved in the past. "Orbit" and "trajectory" are loosely used interchangeably.

It often happens that a subset Y of the state space has the property that states in Y can evolve only to other states in Y, so that if y is any state in Y and $z = \Phi_t(y)$ for some positive or negative t, then necessarily $t \in Y$. Such a set Y is called *invariant*. Every orbit is an invariant set, and every invariant set is a union of orbits. The closure of an invariant set is invariant. Restricting attention to states in an invariant set defines another dynamical system, having a smaller state space but the same rule for computing trajectories.

We also speak of a *positively invariant set*, meaning a set Y with the property that if $y \in Y$ and $t \geq 0$, then $\Phi_t(y) \in Y$. An example is the *forward orbit* of x, which means the set of points $\Phi_t(x), t \geq 0$.

A fundamental dynamical concept is that of a *limit point* of a state x: this means a state $y \in X$ such that $y = \lim_{k \to \infty} \Phi_{t_k}(x)$ for some sequence of times $t_k \to \infty$. It is important to realize that a state can have more than one limit point, because there may be many such sequences $\Phi_{t_k}(x)$ converging to distinct limits.

The set of all limit points of x is called the *limit set* of x (more properly the *omega limit set*), denoted by $\omega(x)$. We also loosely call it the limit set of the trajectory or orbit of x.

If x has a *unique* limit point p, this means that $\Phi_t(x)$ converges to p as $t \to \infty$. In this case p is an equilibrium state (defined below), and we say that the trajectory of x stabilizes at p. I emphasize, however, that for an autonomous reversible system the trajectory of x never actually reaches the state p (that is, p is not on the orbit of x), except in the case that it started at p, that is, when $x = p$.

---

[7] The composition law is proved using the uniqueness theorem for solutions of a differential equation $dx/dt = F(x)$, and the fact that if $x(t)$ is a solution, so is $x(t - b)$ for any constant b.

In the contrary case, a trajectory with more than one limit point wanders around forever near its limit without converging to any definite state.

The following useful facts about limit sets are proved using the composition law and continuity assumptions:

Proposition 3.1   (a) *Every limit set is closed and invariant.*

(b) *A closed, positively invariant set Y contains the limit sets of all states in Y.*

(c) *A state which lies in a compact, positively invariant set K has a limit set which is a nonempty compact subset of K, connected in the continuous-time case.*

A compact nonempty invariant set A is called an *attractor* if it contains the limit sets of all nearby states. More precisely, A is required to have a neighborhood W in the state space such that $\lim_{t \to \infty} d(\Phi_t(x, A)) = 0$, uniformly in $x \in W$. The set of all points whose omega limits are in A is the *basin* of the attractor.

Most dynamical systems used in modelling have a global attractor, i.e. an attractor whose basin is the whole state space. Such systems are termed *dissipative*.

Many dynamic features can be succinctly defined in terms of orbits and limit sets. For example, a *stationary* state or *equilibrium* is a state p which does not change, that is, $\Phi_t(p) = p$ for all t. Equivalently, $\omega(p) = p$.

For a system defined by a vector field F, a state p is an equilibrium if and only if $F(p) = 0$. For a discrete-time system generated by a map $f : X \to X$, the equilibria are the *fixed points* of f, i.e., the states p such that $f(p) = p$.

A state a is *periodic* if $\Phi_r(a) = a$ for some time $r > 0$, called a *period* of a. The limit set of a periodic state coincides with the orbit of the state. If a is periodic but not stationary, the smallest such r is called the *minimal period*, and the orbit of a is called a *cycle*. The composition law implies that if a has period r than so does every state on the orbit of a.

Many useful systems have the property that the limit sets of all (or "most") orbits are equilibria or cycles. It is very important to be able to recognize such systems, since their behavior is reasonably describable; criteria are given in Section 5.1.

But such systems are exceptional! Even very simple-looking systems can have incredibly complicated limit behavior; see the Lorenz system, below. The first such system was discovered a century ago by Poincaré, the inventor of dynamical systems theory, in his study of celestial mechanics [22]. He despaired of describing the dynamic complexity of two planets revolving around the sun under the influence of Newton's laws.

We can now state more precisely the task of dynamical systems theory: to describe the limit sets of the systems we are interested in. More modestly and realistically, we would like to do this for "most" limit sets of "most" such systems. In the present state of knowledge even this is possible only for very special systems, but nevertheless much practical information can be obtained. Even where complete rigor is not attainable, useful insights may be derived.

4 Stability and persistence

A periodic orbit (possibly an equilbrium state) γ is called *topologically stable* if it is an attractor. This means that if we follow the trajectory of any state that is sufficiently close to γ, eventually it will appear to repeat periodically — although in fact it approaches γ asymptotically without actually repeating any state, unless it was in γ to start with.

In particular, an equilibrium can be topologically stable. This notion makes precise the idea of a state to which the system will always return after any sufficiently small disturbance of the state.

There are well-known conditions which are sufficient (but not necessary) for an equilibrium p to be topologically stable. These assume the dynamics are smooth.

Theorem 4.1   (a) *For a discrete-time system defined by a smooth map G : $\mathbf{R}^n \to \mathbf{R}^n$ a fixed point p is topologically stable provided every eigenvalue of $DG(p)$ has absolute value less than 1.*

   (b) *For an autonomous system of differential equations $dx/dt = F(x)$, an equilibrium if p is topologically stable provided every eigenvalue of $Df(p)$ has negative real part.*

These conditions are not necessary, but they are so useful that when they hold then p is simply called *stable* or more precisely, *linearly stable*. The corresponding weak inequalities on eigenvalues can be shown to be necessary (but not sufficient) for topological stability.

Stability of p (as defined by the eigenvalue conditions) implies that nearby orbits can be proved to converge to p at an exponential rate:

Theorem 4.2   (a) *Let p be a stable equilibrium of a smooth vector field F. Suppose every eigenvalue of $DF(p)$ has real part $< -\lambda < 0$. Then there is a constant $C > 0$ and a neighborhood N of p such that $|x(t) - p| \leq C|x(0) - p|e^{-\lambda t}$ for every trajectory $x(t)$ starting in N.*

   (b) *Let p be a stable fixed point of a smooth mapping G. Suppose every eigenvalue of $DG(p)$ has absolute value $< \mu < 1$. Then there is a constant $C > 0$ and a neighborhood N of p such that $|G^k(x) - p| \leq C|x(0) - p|\mu^k$ for every $x \in N$.*

   (c) *There are linear changes of coordinates so that in the new coordinates (a) and (b) are valid with $C = 1$.*

A stable equilibrium enjoys another important type of stability, called *persistence*: If the equations defining the system are subjected to any sufficiently small perturbation, then the perturbed system has a unique equilibrium near p, and it is stable for the perturbed system. In other words a stable equilibrium persists under small changes in the dynamic.

An equilibrium can be persistent without being stable: An example is the fixed point of the map x^3. While unstable equilibria are hard to observe, they exert an important influence on the dynamics because states on nearby orbits change very slowly; this follows from the continuity assumption.

A somewhat weaker kind of stability is the following: Equilibrium p is *orbitally stable* if trajectories starting near p remain near p for all future times. Precisely: for every neighborhood N of p there is a smaller neighborhood W of p which is positively invariant.

A necessary condition for orbital stability of a fixed point p of a smooth mapping F is that every eigenvalue of $DF(p)$ have absolute value less than or equal to 1. For an equilibrium of a smooth vector field H, a necessary condition is that real parts of the eigenvalues of $DH(p)$ be nonpositive.

An equilibrium p of a vector field F is called *simple* if the matrix $DF(p)$ is invertible, or equivalently, 0 is not an eigenvalue. For a map F, an equilibrium (i.e., a fixed point) p is simple if 1 is not an eigenvalue of $DF(p)$. It is generic (see Section 4.2) for all equilibria to be simple. When that is the case, every orbitally stable equilibrium is stable.

A nonequilibrium periodic orbit Γ is *linearly stable* if it is an attractor, and each forward orbit $x(t)$, $t \geq 0$ in its basin is attracted to Γ at an exponential rate:

$$\text{dist}(z(t), \Gamma) \leq C e^{-\lambda t}$$

for positive constants C, λ (depending on $z(0)$). This is equivalent to the condition that all but one eigenvalue of $D\phi_T(p)$ have absolute value < 1, where $T > 0$ is the period of the Γ and p is any point of Γ. Unfortunately it is not known how to ascertain this condition purely from equations of the vector field. Nevertheless it has great theoretical importance.

4.1 Long-term behavior of systems. A dynamical system is *convergent* if every trajectory approaches some equilibrium. More generally, a dynamical system is *quasiconvergent* if every orbit approaches the set of equilibrium states, without necessarily converging to a particular one; such orbits are termed quasiconvergent. This is an unstable situation: it can only happen if the equilibrium set is infinite, but under generic assumptions (see Section 4.2) the number of equilibria is finite. Any smooth dissipative system can be approximated by systems whose equilibria are finite in number. In a simulation a quasiconvergent orbit will appear to converge.

It can happen that the trajectories of almost all states are convergent, or quasiconvergent; here "almost all" is used in the sense of measure theory, meaning "except for a set of initial states having Lebesgue measure zero". Such systems are called *almost convergent*, or *almost quasiconvergent*.

An *oscillatory system* is one for which every limit set is a periodic (perhaps stationary) orbit. The pendulum without friction is an example. The weaker notions of *almost oscillatory*, *quasi-oscillatory*, etc., are defined in the obvious way.

Many systems appear to be oscillatory. It is frequently very difficult to prove they actually are oscillatory; another challenging problem is to identify the mechanism producing the oscillations. Such systems can be produced by coupling individual oscillators.

A system is called *chaotic* if it is very difficult to make reliable long-term predictions for it. Used this way the term is not precise, and in fact there is no generally agreed upon formal definition. Moreover it is exceedingly difficult to verify the formal properties that various writers have proposed for the term. The phrase "sensitive dependence on intial conditions" succinctly conveys the essence of chaotic systems.

A tell-tale sign of chaos is the existence of infinitely many periodic orbits in a bounded region, with unbounded minimal periods. A system that is not almost oscillatory is very likely to be chaotic.

Much of the useful information about the long-term behavior of a system trajectory is contained in the dynamics and geometry of the limit sets. What kinds of limit sets are possible?

We have already discussed periodic limit sets, which are the simplest to understand. Poincaré attributed great importance to periodicity. He conjectured, and C. Pugh and C. Robinson proved [24], that if p is a limit point, the system can be approximated by another system for which p is on a periodic orbit. In practice it is difficult to distinguish between periodic and nonperiodic limit points.

G. D. Birkhoff in [6], one of the founders of dynamical systems theory, wrote:

> From the early times the mind of man has persistently endeavored
> to characterize the motions of the stars by means of periodicities. It
> seems doubtful whether any other mode of satisfactory description

is possible. The intuitive basis for this is easily stated: any motion
of a dynamical system must tend with lapse of time towards a
characteristic cyclic mode of behavior.

Birkhoff was thinking about mechanical systems, but the same intuition is relevant
to the dynamics of all natural systems. It is interesting that today many scientists
do not seem to share his intuition. In any case, taken literally and precisely, his
"intuitive basis" (that all dynamical systems are oscillatory) is false (as well he
knew); but it is true for many systems. The entire development of dynamics can
be viewed as an attempt to find an accurate refinement of Birkhoff's intuition.

Beyond periodic limit sets there are a few well-understood classes of examples,
many intriguing but poorly understood simulations, and an unfortunate amount of
premature talk about the "new science of chaos". Only recently have we begun to
develop concepts and language for describing and dealing with nonperiodic attractors. Not only has very little been rigorously proved, but there is not even a hint
of a structure theory for such attractors.

The important thing to realize is that there *are* exotic limit sets and "strange
attractors", and they are quite common. Many of them are robust: they are not
due to some ingenious choice of coefficients, but on the contrary, they persist under
small perturbations of the system. It is usually impossible, in our current state of
knowledge, to prove that a particular system is chaotic.

By definition, reliable long-term predictions are not possible in such systems. It
is not generally realized that reliable computer simulations are not possible either!
The reason is that at every step of computation, errors are introduced by round-off
and approximation — it is impossible even to enter the number 1/3 accurately
into digital computers which use base 2 for calculations.[8]   In other words, the
simulation of a chaotic system is constantly jumping from one orbit to a nearby
orbit. But "sensitive dependence on initial conditions" means that distinct orbits,
even though they start out close together, eventually diverge. This phenomenon is
easily illustrated with simulations of the *Lorenz system*:

$$\frac{dx}{dt} = -10x + 10y$$
$$\frac{dy}{dt} = 28x - y - xz$$
$$\frac{dz}{dt} = -\frac{8}{3}z + xy.$$

4.2 Generic behavior. An important concept for dynamics is that of
"generic" phenomena, meaning "typical" or "highly probable"; it is closely allied to
notions of stability, persistence and robustness.[9] In a particular system one speaks
of generic states and their trajectories. In dealing with a class of systems one often
discusses generic systems in the class.

In discussing generic behavior one must be careful to specify the class of systems
under consideration. For example one could consider only frictionless pendulums,
for which it is not only generic, but true without exception, that every orbit is
periodic. But for pendulums with friction, only two orbits (the equilibria) are
periodic — generically, orbits are convergent. The meaning of "generic" depends

---

[8]Here the Babylonians, who used base 60, had the advantage.

[9]Like most dynamical ideas this goes back a century to Henri Poincaré: In his work on
celestial mechanics he excluded "infinitely improbable" situations, such as all the planets moving
in a straight line toward the sun.

on the class of systems, and the precise mathematical formulation of "generic". Regrettably there are many such formulations, invented for different situations, and they are not consistent.[10]

But all definitions of "generic" share the following characteristics:

- If a property applicable to members of some topological space S is generic, then the members of S which have the property form a dense subset of S. For example, if S is a space of vector fields and P is some generic property, then any vector field in S can be approximated arbitrarily closely by fields having property P.
- The logical product of any finite or countably infinite set of generic properties is generic.

Many useful generic properties are known, but in these notes we will refer only to the following generic property:

Lemma 4.3 *It is C^k generic, for every $k \geq 1$, for every equilibrium to be simple.*

Unfortunately most rigorously proved generic properties apply only to very large classes, such as the class of all C^k systems for some particular k; and this does not necessarily imply that a particular property will be generic for a smaller class of systems. For example, I don't know if it is generic in some sense for the economic models discussed in this paper to have only simple equilibria (although this is very likely so).

When generic properties are discussed without specifying the class, this usually refers to the class of all C^1 systems.

5 Convergence criteria

The simplest dynamical systems are the convergent ones. It is of prime importance to have at hand convenient criteria for determining whether a given set of equations produces convergent dynamics.

5.1 Liapunov functions. Probably the most useful criterion is the existence of a *Liapunov function*: This means a continuous real-valued function E on the state space which strictly decreases in time along every nonstationary trajectory, and which is bounded from below.[11] Examples: the energy function for mechanical systems with friction; the error function for many automatic learning schemes; negative entropy for statistical mechanical systems.

Consider a smooth continuous-time system $dx/dt = F(x)$ and a smooth real-valued function E on the state space. There is a convenient test for E to be Liapunov: By the chain rule

$$\frac{dE(x(t))}{dt} = DE(x)F(x) = \langle \mathrm{grad}E(x), F(x) \rangle, \tag{5.1}$$

where $\langle u, v \rangle = \sum_i u_i v_i$ denotes the inner (or dot) product of vectors $u, v \in \mathbf{R}^n$. This shows that *E is Liapunov precisely if $\langle \mathrm{grad}E(x), F(x) \rangle < 0$ at all nonstationary states x.* Notice that this algebraic condition can be checked without computing

---

[10]A common definition of a generic property in some complete metric space S is that it defines a subset which contains the intersection of a countable family of open dense sets. Another definition, applicable to measure spaces, is that the property holds for a set whose complement has measure zero. In $\mathbf{R}^n$ the second definition implies the first.

[11]For a dissipative system it is not necessary to assume Liapunov functions are bounded below, as this is automatically satisfied.

solutions of the differential equation. It follows from this condition that *a state p is an equilibrium precisely when it is a critical point for the Liapunov function E*, that is, when $\operatorname{grad} E(p) = 0$.

The most natural class of systems admitting Liapunov functions is the class of *gradient systems*. Such a system is generated by a system of differential equations of the form:

$$\frac{dx_i}{dt} = -\frac{\partial E}{\partial x_i}, \; i = 1, \ldots, n \tag{5.2}$$

or in vector form $dx/dt = -\operatorname{grad} E$. Here it is usually assumed that E is differentiable of class C^2 so that the vector field $-\operatorname{grad} E$ will be C^1, allowing application of the standard theory of differential equations.

It is readily computed that along a solution curve $x(t)$ we have

$$\frac{d}{dt} E(x(t)) = -|\operatorname{grad} E|^2.$$

It follows that E is a Liapunov function.

There is a simple test for determining whether a smooth vector field F on $\mathbf{R}^n$ is the gradient of some function: F is a gradient if and only if all the Jacobian matrices DF are symmetric, i.e., $\partial F_i / \partial x_j = \partial F_j / \partial x_j$.

The main facts about Liapunov functions are as follows:

Theorem 5.1 *Let* $E : X \to \mathbf{R}$ *be a Liapunov function for a dissipative dynamical system* (X, Φ)*. Then:*

- (a) *The system is quasiconvergent, so there are no periodic orbits other than equilibria.*
- (b) *Every local minimum point for E is an orbitally stable equilibrium.*
- (c) *The topologically stable equilibria are exactly the strict local minimum points of E.*
- (d) *The system is convergent in each of the following two cases:*
    - (i) $\operatorname{grad} E = 0$ *at only a finite number of states;*
    - (ii) *the system is the gradient of a real-analytic function.*

Unfortunately there are no general methods for deciding if a system admits a Liapunov function, or for constructing one if it exists.

Sometimes a Liapunov function for a system can be discovered by noting that the system is closely related to a gradient system:

Theorem 5.2 *Let* E *be a smooth function on* $\mathbf{R}^n$*. Let* H *be a vector field of the form*

$$H_i(x) = a_i(x) \frac{\partial E}{\partial x_i} \tag{5.3}$$

where each $a_i : \mathbf{R}^n \to \mathbf{R}$ *is a smooth nonnegative function which is positive wherever* $H \neq 0$*. Then* E *is a Liapunov function for the system*

$$\frac{dx_i}{dt} = -H_i(x). \tag{5.4}$$

Proof First a geometric proof. The vector $-\operatorname{grad} E(x)$, if it is nonzero, is orthogonal to the level surface S of E through x, pointing in the direction of decreasing E. Each component of $-H_i(x)$ is a positive multiple of the corresponding component $-\operatorname{grad} E(x)$. Therefore $-H(x)$ points towards the same side of S. It follows that E decreases on the trajectory of $-H$ through x, since that curve is tangent to $-H(x)$ at x.

Here is a shorter but (to me) less illuminating analytic proof: By the chain rule,

$$\frac{d}{dt}E(x(t)) = -\sum_i \frac{\partial E}{\partial x_i}H_i$$

$$= \sum -a_i(x)\left(\frac{\partial E}{\partial x_i}\right)^2$$

which is negative if $H(x) \neq 0$. □

6 Another economic model

We consider an example similar to that in Section 2, but with a large number n of producers A_i making the same product. Production is now an n-vector $x = (x_i)$. The price of a unit of product is given by an exogenous function $p(s)$, $s = x_1 + \cdots + x_n$. The cost of production to A_i is $C_i(x_i)$. We assume the dynamic is describable by differential equations governing the production rates dx_i/dt.

Each producer wants to increase her profit $\Pi_i = p(x)x_i - C_i(x_i)$, but rather than maximize it, she merely tries to increment it. Thus we assume that x_i is adjusted so as to increase Π_i. Since

$$\frac{d\Pi_i(x(t))}{dt} = \frac{\partial \Pi_i}{\partial x_i}\frac{dx_i}{dt},$$

we postulate:

$$\mathrm{Sign}\,\frac{dx_i}{dt} = \mathrm{Sign}\,\frac{\partial \Pi_i}{\partial x_i}, \tag{6.1}$$

where for any real number s we define $\mathrm{Sign}\,s$ to be $s/|s|$ if $s \neq 0$, and to be 0 if $s = 0$. Therefore we assume there is a positive function $a_i(x)$ such that

$$\frac{dx_i}{dt} = a_i(x)\frac{\partial \Pi_i}{\partial x_i}.$$

Computing $\partial \Pi_i/\partial x_i$ gives us the system of differential equations determining the dynamic:

$$\frac{dx_i}{dt} = a_i(x)[p(x) + p'(x)x_i - C_i'(x_i)]; \ i = 1, \ldots, n. \tag{6.2}$$

Unfortunately this system seems difficult to analyze. We need a simplifying assumption.

There are two assumptions that have mathematically similar effects, but different economic interpretations. One is two assume zero (or constant) costs, so that $C_i' = 0$; we leave this analysis as an exercise. Instead we make the psychological assumption that *producers ignore the effect of their production changes on the price*. In other words they compute $\partial \Pi_i/\partial x_i$ holding p constant. This is not unreasonable if there are very many producers, or if production changes are very small (and here they are infinitesimal!). So instead of system (6.2), we now postulate:

$$\frac{dx_i}{dt} = a_i(x)[p(x_1 + \cdots + x_n) - C_i'(x_i)]; \ i = 1, \ldots, n. \tag{6.3}$$

Notice that an equilibrium of (6.3) is a state x at which all marginal production costs equal the unit price.

System (6.3) is almost a gradient system:

Lemma 6.1 *There is a function* $V : \mathbf{R}^n \to R$ *such that*

$$\frac{\partial V}{\partial x_i} = p(x_1 + \cdots + x_n) - C_i{}'(x_i),$$

and this is > 0 *if* x *is not a constant solution.*

Proof Define

$$V(x_1, \ldots, x_n) = \int_0^s p(r)dr - \sum_i C_i(x_i); \quad s = \sum_i x_i.$$

$\square$

We conclude that trajectories of (6.3) tend to critical points of V.

At this stage we impose a typical "generic" hypothesis (except that we don't know that it is actually generic!): We assume that the function V has only a finite number of critical points (where its gradient vanishes) and that equilibria of (6.3) (which are the critical points of V) are simple. Finally we assume that system (6.3) is dissipative, which means there is a number $R > 0$ such that every solution eventually enters and stays in the ball of radius R about the origin. This is a consequence of plausible assumptions on prices and costs.

It then follows that every solution $x(t)$ is defined for all $t \geq 0$, and approaches an equilibrium as $t \to \infty$. Moreover the assumption of simple equilibria implies that except for a closed set of measure zero, the trajectory of every state converges to a stable equilibrium (which is the same as a local minimum point of $-V$).

This is a powerful conclusion: Every trajectory converges to an equilibrium, and most converge to stable equilibria.

We can learn more by computing the Hessian of $-V$ at any state x: This is the symmetric matrix

$$-DV(x) = -p'E + \text{diag}\, \{C_1{}'', \ldots, C_n{}''\}$$

where E is the $n \times n$ matrix with every entry equal to 1, and "diag" denotes a diagonal matrix.

We assume for simplicity that all production rates x_i are positive at equilibria.[12]

If e is an equilibrium, then it is stable if and only if all the eigenalues of $-DV(e)$ are negative. A standard result in matrix theory, Gerschgorin's Theorem[13] [**19**], implies:

Lemma 6.2 *The eigenvalues of* $-DV(e)$ *are negative provided that*

$$\max_i C_i{}''(e_i) < np' \left(\sum e_i \right).$$

If this condition holds at every equilibrium, then there is only one equilibrium.[14]

We can interpret Lemma 6.2 as follows. Since $C_i{}''$ is the rate of change of marginal demand with respect to supply, and p' is the rate of change with respect to price, we conclude:

---

[12]This assumption can be interpreted as the assumption of a mature economy, in which only profit-making firms have survived. But in fact the phenomenon of firms leaving and entering the economy is a difficult one to treat dynamically, as it changes the dimension of the state space.

[13]Gerschgorin's Theorem for a real or complex square matrix A states that for each i there is an eigenvalue in the closed disc centered at A_{ii} with radius $\sum_{j, j \neq i} |A_{ij}|$.

[14]The basins of distinct stable equilibria are disjoint open sets. But the state space is connected– it cannot be the union of disjoint nonempty open sets. Therefore if every equilibrium is stable there can be only one equilibrium.

If increasing production causes marginal costs to decrease sufficiently more rapidly than demand, then System (6.3) is globally convergent.

Assuming that a globally convergent market system is desirable (which is by no means clear), how could it be established? One possibility is for the government to tax revenues at a sufficiently high rate r, $0 < r < 1$. In this case profits are recomputed as

$$\Pi_i = (1-r)px_i - C_i,$$

so holding p constants gives

$$d\Pi_i/dx_i = (1-r)p - C_i'.$$

Instead of (6.3) we have:

$$\frac{dx_i}{dt} = a_i(x)[(1-r)p(x_1 + \cdots + x_n) - C_i'(x_i)]; \ i = 1, \ldots, n. \tag{6.4}$$

As before there is a Liapunov function.

The Jacobian matrix at an equilibrium of the vector field defined by (6.4) is:

$$\text{diag}\{a_i\}[(1-r)p'E - \text{diag}\{C_1'', \ldots, C_n''\}].$$

Gershgorin's Theorem implies stability of equilibria, and hence global convergence to a unique equilibrium, in case

$$\max_i C_i'' < (1-r)np' \tag{6.5}$$

at every equilibrium. Evidently this can be achieved by a tax rate r which is sufficiently confiscatory (close to 1).

By allowing the positive function a_i in (6.3) to depend on time we sacrifice autonomy of the system of ODEs, but we allow the interpretation that producers can make different production choices at different times, even under identical market conditions. This leads to the slightly nonautonomous system

$$\frac{dx_i}{dt} = a_i(x,t)[p(x_1 + \cdots + x_n) - C_i'(x_i)]; \ i = 1, \ldots, n. \tag{6.6}$$

The nonautonomy is not serious because one can show that the same function V is Liapunov for (6.4), in the sense that it decreases along nonconstant solutions. Under the further assumption that every point x has a neighborhood U such that

$$\inf\{a_i(x,t) : x \in U, t \geq 0\} > 0,$$

one can prove that every solution tends toward a critical point of V.

7 Monotone dynamics

The *vector order* in $\mathbf{R}^n$ is the partial order relation defined by:

$$x \leq y \Leftrightarrow x_i \leq y_i, \ i = 1, \ldots, n.$$

A dynamical system is called *monotone* if it preserves this order for positive time. If the dynamic is Φ, this means that

$$t \geq 0, x \leq y \Rightarrow \Phi_t(x) \leq \Phi_t(y).$$

Such systems have very special dynamical properties, yet they arise in many situations. Before giving examples in the following sections, we state some results about them.

A C^1 vector field F in $\mathbf{R}^n$ is *cooperative* (or *quasimonotone*) if $\partial F_i/\partial x_j \geq 0$ whenever $i \neq j$.

Theorem 7.1 (MÜLLER-KAMKE) *The solution flow of a cooperative vector field is monotone.*

Proof See the book by Coppel [8].   □

An $n \times n$ matrix M is *irreducible* if for every partition of the set $\{1, \dots , n\}$ into two disjoint nonempty subsets S, T, for any $i \in S$ there exists $j \in T$ with $M_{ij} \neq 0$.

A vector field is called irreducible if its Jacobian matrices are irreducible.

The following result shows that cooperative dynamical systems have very special dynamics, namely, generic orbits are quasiconvergent:

Theorem 7.2 *Consider the dynamics of a cooperative vector field F in $\mathbf{R}^n$.*

(a) *Every attractor contains an orbitally stable equilibrium. In particular there are no attracting periodic orbits.*

(b) *Suppose F is irreducible. Then there is a dense invariant set X whose complement has measure zero, such that every bounded forward trajectory in X is convergent. If the set of equilibria is countable (or finite), then every bounded trajectory in X is convergent.*

(c) *Suppose $n = 2$. Then every bounded forward or backward trajectory converges.*

Proof Part (a) can be derived from Hirsch in [13]. Part (c) is proved by Hadeler and Glas in [11]; see also Hirsch [14] . Versions of part (b) have been proved by several authors: Smith and Thieme [27], Polàčik [23], Takáč [20]. See also Hirsch [15].   □

There are examples satisfying the hypotheses of Theorem 7.2 that have arbitrarily complex dynamics in invariant subsets — but these sets have measure zero, and cannot be attractors. Such examples show that we cannot expect general cooperative systems to have Liapunov functions.

A vector field F in $\mathbf{R}^n$ is called *competitive* if it is C^1 and the off-diagonal terms of Jacobian matrices are ≤ 0; this is equivalent to $-F$ being cooperative. S. Smale in [26] showed that an arbitrary system of ODEs in $\mathbf{R}^{n-1}$ can be embedded as an attractor in a competitive system in $\mathbf{R}^n$, so this is not a very powerful assumption from a general dynamical point of view. For two dimensions, however, we have the following result:

Theorem 7.3 *Let $x(t)$, $0 < t < \infty$ be a bounded trajectory of a competitive vector field in $\mathbf{R}^2$. Then there is an equilibrium e such that $x(t) \to e$, with each component converging monotonically (nonincreasing or nondecreasing).*

In fact Theorem 7.3 and Theorem 7.2(c) are valid for slightly nonautonomous systems of the form:

$$\frac{dx_i}{dt} = a_i(x, t) G_i(x), \; i = 1, 2 \tag{7.1}$$

where the functions a_i are positive, and the vector field G is competitive (for Theorem 7.3) or cooperative (for Theorem 7.2(c)).

We turn now to monotone discrete time systems. It is not hard to show that a C^1 map F from a convex subset of $\mathbf{R}^n$ to $\mathbf{R}^n$ is monotone provided all its partial derivatives are nonnegative. The following result is an analog of Theorem 7.2(a); it can be derived from Hirsch [12], [13]:

Theorem 7.4 *Let $X \subset \mathbf{R}^n$ denote either $\mathbf{R}^n$, an orthant of $\mathbf{R}^n$, or an $n-$cube. Let $F : X \to X$ be a continuous monotone map which defines a dissipative dynamical system. Then:*

(a) *F has an orbitally stable fixed point.*
(b) *Every attractor contains an orbitally stable periodic orbit.*

This shows that an attractor A in such a system cannot be very chaotic: If A is not a finite set, no orbit is dense in A, nor can a union of periodic orbits be dense in A — properties often used to define chaos.

8 A cooperative model of competition

Here we consider another of X. Vives' oligopoly games, this time "Bertrand competition in differentiated markets".

Let there be n producers $\mathcal{A}_i$ producing products which are gross substitutes. $\mathcal{A}_i$ continually adjusts the price p_i of her product. The demand for the i'th product is a positive function $h_i(p)$ of the price vector $p = (p_i)$. $\mathcal{A}_i$ produces exactly enough to meet the demand. The production cost of the i'th good is $C_i(h_i(p))$. The profit to $\mathcal{A}_i$ is $\Pi_i = p_i h_i - C_i$.

Each agent acts so as to increase profits. We interpret this to mean that there are positive functions $a_i(p_i)$ such that

$$dp_i/dt = a_i(p_i)\partial\Pi_i/\partial p_i.$$

This time we assume that our oligopolists understand perfectly the effect of price changes on demands and costs. Computing $\partial\Pi_i/\partial p_i$ yields the following dynamical system, whose state space is the space of price vectors p:

$$\frac{dp_i}{dt} = a_i(p_i)[\{p_i - C_i{}'(h_i(p))\}\frac{\partial h_i(p)}{\partial p_i} + h_i(p)] := F_i(p). \qquad (8.1)$$

We make the natural assumptions $\partial h_i/\partial p_i < 0$ and $C_i{}' > 0$.

The following additional mathematical assumptions are made to guarantee that vector field F is cooperative; we attempt to interpret them economically. First of all, as the products are gross substitutes we have:

(i) $\dfrac{\partial h_i}{\partial p_j} > 0$ for $i \neq j$.

We postulate what has been called "submodularity" in a related context ([**28**], [**29**]):

(ii) Suppose all prices are held fixed except for p_i. Let $j \neq i$. At a higher level of p_j, the marginal demand for good i with respect to p_i greater than at a lower level of p_j:

$$\frac{\partial}{\partial p_j}(\frac{\partial h_i}{\partial p_i}) \geq 0.$$

We also need to assume:

(iii)

$$C_i{}''\frac{\partial h_i}{\partial p_i} < 1.$$

To interpret (iii), suppose all prices, demands and costs are fixed except those for good i. Ignoring the other goods and recalling that $\partial h_i/\partial p_i < 0$, we see that (iii) is equivalent to

$$\frac{dC_i{}'}{dh_i} > \frac{dp_i}{dh_i}.$$

If we identify h_i with the production and hence the supply of good i, this says that as supply increases, marginal cost does not fall as quickly as price. Note that (iii) holds in the special case of linear costs.

Finally we make the drastic hypothesis that producers choose prices which at least equal marginal costs:

(iv) $p_i - C_i' \geq 0$.

This holds, for example, if there are only fixed costs ($C_i' = 0$).

Lemma 8.1 *Under assumptions (i)—(iv), System (8.1) is cooperative and irreducible.*

Proof   A computation yields, for $i \neq j$:

$$\frac{\partial F_i}{\partial p_j} = a_i \left[(p_i - C_i') \frac{\partial^2 h_i}{\partial h_j \partial h_i} + \left(1 - \frac{\partial h_i}{\partial p_i} C_i'' \right) \frac{\partial h_i}{\partial p_j} \right]. \tag{8.2}$$

Coefficient a_i is positive, the first summand is nonnegative by (iv) and (ii), and the second is positive by (iii) and (i). Therefore Jacobian matrices of F have positive off-diagonal terms.   □

Applying Theorem 7.2 we obtain:

Theorem 8.2 *Under assumptions (i)—(iv), there is a dense invariant set X having full measure, such that every bounded forward trajectory approaches the set of equilibria.*

9 The simple model revisited

We consider again the mapping in Section 2

$$F : \mathbf{R}_+^2 \to \mathbf{R}_+^2,$$

having the form

$$F(x_1, x_2) = (f_1(x_2), f_2(x_1))$$

with

$$f_i' < 0, \; i = 1, 2.$$

This system is dissipative, but not monotone. It can be made monotone, however, by the simple coordinate change

$$\begin{aligned} y_1 &= x_1, \\ y_2 &= -x_2. \end{aligned}$$

In these coordinates the dynamic is given by the map

$$G : X \to X, \; X = \{ y \in \mathbf{R}^2 : y_1 \geq 0, \, y_2 \leq 0 \}$$

where

$$\begin{aligned} G(y_1, y_2) &= (g_1(y_2), g_2(y_1)), \\ g_1(y_2) &= f_1(-y_2), \\ g_2(y_1) &= -f_2(y_1). \end{aligned}$$

Then $g_i' > 0$, implying that G is monotone.

Now we apply Theorem 7.4 to G, to conclude that G has an orbitally stable fixed point. Reverting to the original system, we have:

Theorem 9.1 *The system F has an orbitally stable fixed point.*

Under the (hopefully) generic assumption of simple fixed points, there is a stable fixed point.

10 Stochastic allocation processes and deterministic dynamics

In this section and the next we consider discrete-time systems where the current state of the system determines not the next state, but rather the *probability distribution* of the next state. We suppose further that as time goes on, the probability of any particular state change goes to zero.

Example 10.1 (Allocation Processes) Paraphrasing B. Arthur [1]: Suppose a unit addition or allocation is made to one of d categories at each time, with probabilities that are a function of the proportion of units currently in the categories. Time here is event time, not clock time. In practice we might be considering the build-up of market shares by observing the "allocation" of adopters, one at a time, to d technologies; or consumers to d product brands; or, in regional economics, firms to d locations. Thus, the next unit is added to category i with probability $g_i(x)$ where $x = (x_1, \ldots, x_d)$ is the vector of current proportions or market shares. Here g is a deterministic, exogenously given map of the $d-1$ simplex Δ^{d-1} into itself:

$$g : \Delta^{d-1} \to \Delta^{d-1},$$

$$\Delta^{d-1} = \left\{ x = (x_1, \ldots, x_d) \in \mathbf{R}^d : 0 \le x_i \le 1, \ \sum_{i=1}^{d} x_i = 1. \right\}$$

We start the process at time $k = 0$ with an initial vector $y = (y_1, \ldots, y_d)$ of allocations, and initial total allocation $w = \sum y_i > 0$. The initial vector $x_0 \in \Delta^{d-1}$ has components $x_0(i) = y_i/w$. At time $k \in \mathbf{N}$ we have allocated $w + (k-1)$ units. If $Y_k \in \mathbf{R}^d$ denotes the vector of allocations, then the vector of proportions is $x_k = Y_k/(w + k - 1)$. We select an integer $j_{k+1} \in \{1, \ldots, d\}$ at random, the probability that $j_{k+1} = i$ being $g_i(x(k))$. We then increase the allocation to category $j(k)$ by one unit. Let e_{k+1} denote the random unit vector whose $i'th$ coordinate is 1 if $i = j_{k+1}$ and 0 otherwise. Then

$$x_{k+1} = x_k + \frac{1}{w+k+1}(e_{k+1} - x_k) \tag{10.1}$$

We rewrite this as

$$x_{k+1} = x_k + \frac{1}{w+k+1}(g(x_k) - x_k) + \frac{1}{w+k+1}(e_{k+1} - x_k). \tag{10.2}$$

Now it is easy to see that the conditional expectation of the random variable $U_{k+1} = e_{k+1} - x_k$, given the current state x_k, is 0. We emphasize this by rewriting Equation (10.2) as

$$x_{k+1} = x_k + \frac{1}{w+k+1}(g(x_k) - x_k + U_{k+1}), \tag{10.3}$$

with

$$\mathsf{E}(U_{k+1}|x_k) = 0. \tag{10.4}$$

From this it is easy to calculate the expected value of x_{k+1} given the current state:

$$\mathsf{E}(x_{k+1}|x_k) = \frac{1}{w+k+1}(g(x_k) - x_k). \tag{10.5}$$

There is a strong resemblance between Equation (10.3) and the Cauchy-Euler approximation to the solution of the differential equation[15]

$$\frac{dx}{dt} = g(x) - x; \tag{10.6}$$

with variable stepsize $\frac{1}{w+k+1}$:

$$x_{k+1} = x_k + \frac{1}{w+k+1}(g(x_k) - x_k). \tag{10.7}$$

Thus Equation (10.3) can be viewed as the result of a noisy numerical solution to Equation (10.6).

It is thus reasonable to expect a close relationship between the limit $L\{x_k\}$ of a sample path $\{x_k\}$ of Equation (10.3) (i.e., the set of limit points of subsequences) and limit sets of solutions of Equation (10.6). Such a relationship has long been known in case the dynamics of Equation (10.3) are very simple, for example of gradient type, or globally convergent (see the books by Benveniste et al. [5] and Kushner and Clark [18]).

Recently a very general result has been proved by M. Benaïm [2]. To state this result we need the following dynamical concept. A set $L \subset \Delta^{d-1}$ is called *internally chain transitive* for Equation (10.3) if it has the following properties:

(i) L is nonempty, compact and connected,
(ii) L is invariant: it contains the complete solution curve through every point of L,
(iii) $\forall \epsilon > 0, T > 0$ we can pass from any point of L to any other point by following orbits in L and allowing, at times separated by at least T, a finite number of jumps of size $< \epsilon$ to other orbits in L.

An equivalent definition is that the flow defined in L defined by following solution curves to Equation (10.3) has no proper attracting or repelling sets.

It can be shown that if F has a Liapunov function, and only finitely many equilibria, then the only internally chain transitive sets are equilibria. Likewise for a vector field in the plane with negative divergence almost everywhere. In general, however, internally chain transitive sets can be very complicated.

The following is a special case of the main result of Benaïm [2]:

Theorem 10.2 *Assume the map g is Lipschitz (e.g., continuously differentiable). Then with probability one, the limit set $L\{x_k\}$ of a sample path $\{x_k\}$ of process Equation (10.3) is internally chain transitive for Equation (10.6).*

In favorable circumstances we can therefore derive information about the allocation process (10.3) from the dynamics of the vector field F in Δ^{d-1} representing the right-hand side of Equation (10.6). This idea was exploited by Benaïm and Hirsch in [3]. A simple example:

---

[15]Here we regard the map $x \mapsto g(x) - x$ as a vector field $f : \Delta^{d-1} \to T\Delta^{d-1}$ on Δ^{d-1} with values in the *tangent space* to Δ^{d-1}, namely the linear subspace of $\mathbf{R}^d$ defined by

$$T\Delta^{d-1} = \left\{ x \in \mathbf{R}^d : \sum x_i = 0 \right\}.$$

If we identify Δ^{d-1} with a simplex $\sigma^{d-1} \subset \mathbf{R}^{d-1}$ by a convenient affine homeomorphism, then f is a vector field on σ^{d-1}.

Corollary 10.3 *Assume that system (10.6) has a Liapunov function, and that every trajectory converges to one of a finite set of equilibria. Then with probability one, a sample path of the allocation process (10.3) converges to one of these equilibria.*

11 Urn processes

Stochastic processes such as Equation (10.3) are examples of *generalized Polya urn processes*. In this interpretation, an urn initially contains w balls of $d \geq 2$ different colors. At stage k we add one new ball whose color is chosen as follows. Let $x_k \in \Delta^{d-1}$ be the vector whose $i'th$ coordinate is the proportion of balls of color i currently in the urn. Then the probability that we add a ball of color i is $g_i(x_k)$. It is not hard to see that Equations (10.3), (10.4) and (10.5) describe the evolution of the process $\{x_k\}$. Thus Theorem 10.2 applies to these urn processes.

Much more can be said about the relation between sample paths and dynamics. One can ask, for example, whether a given equilibrium is likely to be the limit set of a sample path, or more generally, whether a given internally chain transitive set has positive probability of containing the limit set. The following theorem states some results proved in [21] and [3]:

Theorem 11.1 *Assume that g in Equation (10.6) is C^2.*

(a) *If w is a linearly stable equilibrium then*

$$\mathsf{P}\{\lim z_k = w\} > 0;$$

(b) *If w is a linearly unstable equilibrium then*

$$\mathsf{P}\{\lim z_k = w\} = 0.$$

(c) *If Γ is a linearly unstable periodic orbit then*

$$\mathsf{P}\{L\{x_k\} \cap \Gamma \neq \emptyset\} = 0.$$

(d) *Assume g maps Δ^{d-1} into its interior (g need only be Lipschitz now.) If Λ is an attractor then*

$$\mathsf{P}\{L\{x_k \subset \Lambda\} > 0.$$

Suppose there is no reason to expect orbits of Equation (10.6) to converge; the system may be thought to be oscillatory or chaotic, for example. We may then inquire whether sample paths are likely to closely track trajectories. The following result, a consequence of [2], gives conditions under which this is true.

In order to state this result we introduce an numerical invariant called the *logarithmic expansion rate* $l_{\exp}(F)$ of the vector field F on Δ^{d-1}, which is hard to compute but often easy to estimate. Let $\{\Phi_t\}_{t \in \mathbf{R}}$ denote the flow generated by Equation (10.3). Then

$$l_{\exp}(F) = \liminf_{t \to \infty} \min_{x \in \Delta^{d-1}} \frac{1}{t} ||(D\Phi_t(x))^{-1}||^{-1}.$$

If $l_{\exp}(F) > -c$ for some $c \geq 0$ then it can be shown that for all sufficiently large $t > 0$, the map Φ_t has the following property. For sufficiently small $r > 0$,

$$\Phi_t B(x, r) \subset B(\Phi_t x, e^{-ct} r)$$

where $B(x, r)$ denotes the set of points in Δ^{d-1} at distance $\leq r$ from $x \in \Delta^{d-1}$.

In [16] I gave several estimates for $l_{\exp}(F)$, including the following:

(a)
$$l_{\exp}(F) \geq \inf_x \beta(x), \tag{11.1}$$

where $\beta(x)$ denotes the smallest eigenvalue of the matrix

$$\frac{1}{2}(DF(x) + DF(x))^T.$$

(b) If F is Morse-Smale and $\gamma \in \mathbf{R}$ is the smallest characteristic exponent of periodic and stationary orbits, then

$$l_{\exp}(F) \geq \gamma. \tag{11.2}$$

In the following consequence of a theorem of Benaïm, we assume given an urn process (10.3) and the corresponding dynamical system (10.6) with vector field $F(x) = g(x) - x$. Set

$$\tau_n = \tau(n) = \sum_1^n \frac{1}{w+n}.$$

It is easy to see that there exists $\beta > 0$ and a sequence $\epsilon_n \to 0$ such that

$$\tau_n = \log(w+n) + \beta + \epsilon_n. \tag{11.3}$$

Theorem 11.2 *Assume*

$$l_{\exp}(F) = -c > -\frac{1}{2}.$$

Then with probability one there is a random variable y in Δ^{d-1} with the following property:

$$\lim_{n \to \infty} ||x_n - \Phi(\tau_n, y)|| = 0. \tag{11.4}$$

This means that there is solution $u(t)$ to Equation (10.6) such that the sequence $\{u_{\tau(n)}\}$ is asymptotic with the sample path $\{x_n\}$.

The initial value $u(0)$ is the random variable y, and cannot be computed in most cases. Nevertheless this result tells us that the sample path closely follows *some* trajectory of Equation (10.6) — albeit with a slowing down of time (the difference between the sequences $\{n\}$ and $\{\tau_n\}$.

One can construct generalized Polya urns — or allocation processes — with novel long run behavior by exploiting Theorem 11.2. Suppose for example that H is a C^2 vector field on Δ^2 which points transversely inward on the boundary, has a linearly unstable repelling equilibrium b in the interior, and a unique nonstationary periodic orbit Γ which is linearly stable and which attracts all forward orbits except b. For sufficiently $\epsilon > 0$ the map $g : x \mapsto x + \epsilon H(x)$ sends Δ^2 into its interior. The urn process (10.3) with $g = g_\epsilon$ corresponds to the vector field $\epsilon h(x)$ via Equation (10.6). By (11.1) we choose $\epsilon > 0$ sufficiently small that

$$l_{\exp}(\epsilon H) > -\frac{1}{2}.$$

Theorem 11.3 *Let g_ϵ be as above and consider sample paths $\{x_n\}$ of the 3-color urn process (10.3) with $g = g_\epsilon$. Then with probability one there is a unique periodic trajectory $z : \mathbf{R} \to \Gamma$ of h_ϵ such that*

$$\lim_{n \to \infty} ||x_n - z(\log(w+n))|| = 0. \tag{11.5}$$

Proof It is well known, however, that any trajectory in the basin of a linearly stable periodic orbit Γ is asymptotic with a trajectory $z(t)$ in Γ (Hirsch and Smale [**17**]; see Hirsch [**16**] for generalizations). Therefore from Theorem 11.2 we conclude that almost surely there exists $y \in \Gamma$ satisfying Equation (11.4) for the process under consideration. The theorem now follows from Equation (11.3) by choosing the initial value of $z(t)$ to be $\Phi_\beta y$.   □

In a similar construction one can start from a vector field H in the 4-simplex for which all trajectories except for a linearly unstable equilibrium are attracted to a chaotic trajectory, and thereby construct an urn model for which sample paths almost surely track chaotic trajectories.

12 Repeated randomized games and deterministic dynamics

Consider a game played repeatedly by two players, each having 2 pure strategies, called here *actions*. At play k she chooses her pure strategy to maximize her expected payoff, under the natural but mistaken assumption that her opponent plays the mixed strategy corresponding to her past frequencies of pure strategies. To formalize this, let N_k be the number of times that the second player has played strategy 1 in the first k games. The *empirical frequency vector* of player 2 after play k is:

$$q_k = (y_k, 1 - y_k) \in \Delta^1, \; y_k = \frac{1}{k}\sum_{j=1}^{k} N_j.$$

The empirical frequency vectors $p_k = (x_k, 1 - x_k)$ of player 1 are defined similarly. Let $q_0 = (y_0, 1 - y_0), p_0 = (x_0, 1 - x_0)$ be arbitrary vectors in Δ^1.

Let player 1 have the 2×2 payoff matrix A, so that A_{lm} is her payoff if she and her opponent play $l, m \in \{1, 2\}$ respectively.

Player 1 assumes at play $k+1$ that her opponent will play the mixed strategy q_k, so she plays the action which maximizes her expected payoff under this assumption: At play $k + 1$ she plays strategy $l \in \{1, 2\}$, where

$$l = \text{argmax}_{m \in \{1,2\}} (Aq_k)_m, \tag{12.1}$$

with any convenient rule for the cases where the argmax is not unique. Player 2, with payoff matrix B, behaves similarly. These behavior rules constitute what is called *fictitious play* (Brown [**7**], Robinson [**25**]).

Thus far we have a deterministic system. We now assume, however, that the payoff matrices change in a random way. The first player's payoff matrix for game k has the form $A_k = A + E_k$ where $\{E_k\}_{k \in \mathbf{N}}$ is a sequence of independent, identically distributed, matrix-valued random variables with common mean zero. We assume each entry $E_{k,lm}$ lies in a finite interval, and has a probability distribution given by a smooth (continuously differentiable) density function supported on that interval; and that different entries are independent random variables. The second player's payoff is given by a similar sequence of random matrices $B_k = B + F_k$.

We assume for each k: *at the beginning of play k each player knows her own payoff matrix, and her opponent's empirical frequency vector*. Again each player chooses the action which maximizes her expected payoff under the assumption that her opponent plays the mixed strategy given by her empirical frequency vector. Thus player 1 plays action $l_k \in \{1, 2\}$ given by

$$l_k = \text{argmax}_{m \in \{1,2\}} (A_k q_k)_m, \tag{12.2}$$

while player 2 plays strategy

$$m_k = \mathrm{argmax}_{m \in \{1,2\}} (B_k p_k)_m. \tag{12.3}$$

It can be shown that the assumptions on the E_k imply that, with probability one, (12.2) and (12.3) specify unique strategies.

The *state* of the game immediately after play $k \geq 1$ is defined to be the vector $z_k = (x_k, y_k) \in \Delta^1 \times \Delta^1$ specifying the empirical frequencies with which each player has chosen strategy 1; the initial state is the arbitrary vector $(x_0, y_0) \in \Delta^1 \times \Delta^1$. Because of randomness in the payoff matrices, the sequence $\{z_k\}_{k \in \mathbf{N}}$ is a stochastic process.

We now calculate the conditional expected value of z_{k+1} given z_k. We do this for the first component x_{k+1}, the second component being similar. Fix k and set $E_{k,ij} = E_{ij}$. Let P_k denote conditional probability given z_k. Then from the definition of x_k we have

$$(k+1)x_{k+1} = kx_k + X_{k+1} \tag{12.4}$$

where $X_{k+1} \in \{0, 1\}$ is a random variable such that:

$$
\begin{aligned}
\mathsf{P}_k\{X_{k+1} = 1\} &= \mathsf{P}_k\{(A_k q_k)_1 > (A_k q_k)_2\} \\
&= \mathsf{P}_k\{E_{11}y_k + E_{12}(1 - y_k) > E_{21}y_k + E_{22}(1 - y_k)\} \\
&= \mathsf{P}_k\{y_k(E_{11} - E_{12} - E_{21} + E_{22}) > E_{22} - E_{12}\}, \\
\mathsf{P}_k\{X_{k+1} = 1\} &= g(y_k), \tag{12.5}
\end{aligned}
$$

where g is a smooth bounded function which can be computed from the probability densities of the E_{ij}. Therefore from Equation (12.4) we derive:

$$\mathsf{E}(x_{k+1}|z_k) = x_k + \frac{1}{k+1}(-x_k + g(y_k)). \tag{12.6}$$

Now define a random variable V_{k+1} by the equation

$$\frac{V_{k+1}}{k+1} = x_{k+1} - \mathsf{E}(x_{k+1}|z_k); \tag{12.7}$$

then V_{k+1} is bounded (independently of k), and has mean zero conditional on z_k. From (12.6) and (12.7) we obtain

$$x_{k+1} = x_k + \frac{1}{k+1}(-x_k + V_{k+1});$$

an analogous formula relates y_{k+1} and y_k. Finally we obtain the key recursion:

$$z_{k+1} = z_k + \frac{1}{k+1}(-z_k + h(z_k) + U_{k+1}) \tag{12.8}$$

where the smooth map $h : [0, 1] \times [0, 1] \to \mathbf{R} \times \mathbf{R}$ has the form

$$h(x, y) = (g_1(y), g_2(x)), \tag{12.9}$$

and $\{U_{k+1}\}_{k \in \mathbf{N}}$ is a bounded sequence of mean-zero random variables with values in $\mathbf{R}^2$, such that

$$\mathsf{E}(U_{k+1}|z_k) = 0;$$

in technical jargon they are martingale differences.

The theorem of Benaïm is applicable here: *almost surely the limit set $L\{z_k\}$ of a sample path $\{z_k\}$ is an internally chain transitive set for the flow of the differential* *equation:*

$$\frac{dx}{dt} = -x + g_1(y) \tag{12.10}$$

$$\frac{dy}{dt} = -y + g_2(x). \tag{12.11}$$

What information can we get from this? There are two steps: First, investigate internally chain transitive sets for this system; second, interpret them in terms of the stochastic process.

The first thing to observe is that the vector field

$$F(x,y) = (-x + g_1(y), -y + g_2(x)) \tag{12.12}$$

representing the right-hand side of Equation (12.12) is negative. This implies, by standard theory, that the solution flow (defined by following solution curves) decreases areas. This leads to the conclusion that *every internally chain transitive set is a nonempty compact connected set of equilibria.* An equilbrium means a fixed point of the flow, or equivalently, a vector (x, y) such that $F(x, y) = (0,0)$. From the formula for $F(x, y)$ we see that the set of equilibria is just the intersection of the graphs $x = g_1(y)$ and $y = g_2(x)$. The only compact connected nonempty subsets of the graph of a smooth function are points and smooth arcs. Thus we conclude: *with probability one, sample paths limit at either a point or a smooth arc.*

Since generically, in some sense, two smooth graphs intersect at isolated points, we are strongly tempted to conclude: "generically, almost surely the sequence of empirical frequencies of each player converges". To justify this rigorously, however, would require showing that this conclusion holds for a "generic" set of density functions for the payoff matrices. This is an interesting question which is probably not too difficult to decide one way or the other. Part of the problem is to specify the precise meaning of "generic".

Regardless of genericity, we can conclude:

Theorem 12.1 *If the vector field F has only isolated zeroes, then almost surely the sequences of empirical frequencies converge.*

By a finer analysis (Benaïm and Hirsch [4]) one can prove:

Theorem 12.2 *Assume that the functions g_1 and g_2 are strictly positive and have continuous second derivatives, and that at every equilibrium the Jacobian determinant of F is nonzero. Then almost surely the following hold:*

(a) *The sequence $\{z_k\}$ of empirical frequency vectors converge to an equilibrium of F;*

(b) *if w is a linearly stable equilibrium then*

$$P\{\lim z_k = w\} > 0;$$

(c) *if w is a linearly unstable equilibrium then*

$$P\{\lim z_k = w\} = 0.$$

Suppose every equilibrium of F is either linearly stable or linearly unstable — this is generic for vector fields, and probably generic for the probability distributions under consideration. Then, as the set S of linearly stable equilibria is finite, it follows that with probability one, sample paths converge to an element of the finite set S.

The following result, left as an exercise, is also of interest:

Proposition 12.3 *Assume (in addition to the earlier assumptions):*

(a) *the probability densities of the entries in the random matrices E_k and F_k are real analytic in the interiors of their support intervals,*

(b) *There exists $0 < s < 1$ such that $f(g(s)) \neq s$.*

Then the equilibrium set $\mathcal{E}$ of F is finite, and with probability one, sample paths converge to elements of $\mathcal{E}$.

We can give a game-theoretic interpretation to an equilibrium (u_1, u_2) of the game vector field. Denote by U_i the random matrix variable which has the same distribution as the payoff matrix for player $i \in \{1, 2\}$ for any game $k \in \mathbf{N}$ (these have identical distributions for all k). Following [9] we define a *Nash distribution equilibrium* to be a vector $u = (u_1, u_2) \in \Delta^1 \times \Delta^1$ with the following property for both choices of $i, j \in \{1, 2\}$, $i \neq j$: If $l_j = l_j(U_j, u_i) \in \{1, 2\}$ is the action which maximizes the expected payoff to player j, assuming that player i plays mixed strategy $(u_i, 1 - u_i)$, then it is required that u_j be the expected value of the random variable l_j.

From the definition (12.12), (12.5) of the game vector field F there follows:

Theorem 12.4 $u \in \Delta^1 \times \Delta^1$ *is an equilibrium of the game vector field if and only if u is a Nash distribution equilibrium.*

Applications to Prisoners Dilemma and other games are given in Benaïm and Hirsch [4].

References

[1] Arthur, B. [1988], *Self-reinforcing mechanisms in economics*, in The Economy as an Evolving Complex System (P. W. Anderson, K. J. Arrow, and D. Pines eds.), Addison-Wesley, pp. 10–31.

[2] Benaïm, M. [1996], *A dynamical system approach to stochastic approximation*, Siam Journal of Optimisation and Control **34**, 437-472.

[3] Benaïm, M. and Hirsch, M. W. [1993], *Dynamics of morse-smale urn processes*, Mathematics Department, U. California at Berkeley, Technical Report. Ergodic Theory and Dynamical Systems **15**, 1005-1030.

[4] Benaïm, M. and Hirsch, M. W. [1994], *Learning processes, mixed equilibria and dynamical systems arising from repeated games*, Mathematics Department, University of California at Berkeley, preprint. Submitted.

[5] Benveniste, A., Métivier, M. and Priouret, P. [1990], *Stochastic Approximations and Adaptive Algorithms*, Springer, Berlin, Heidelberg, New York. Translated from: *Algorithmes adaptatifs et approximations stochastiques*, Masson, Paris 1987.

[6] Birkhoff, G. D. [1920], *Recent advances in dynamics*, Science **51**, 51–55.

[7] Brown, G. W. [1951], *Iterative solutions of games by fictitious play*, in Activity Analysis of Production and Allocation (T. C. Koopmans, ed.), Wiley, New York.

[8] Coppel, W. A. [1965], *Stability and asymptotic behavior of differential equations*, Heath, Boston.

[9] Fudenberg, D. and Kreps, K. [1993], *Learning mixed equilibria*, Games and Economic Behavior **5**, 320–367.

[10] Gori, F., Geronazzo, L. and Galeotti, M. [1993], (editors), *Nonlinear Dynamics in Economics and Social Sciences*, Springer, Berlin, Heidelberg, New York. Second Informal Workshop at Certosa di Pontignano, Siena, Italy, May 27-30, 1991.

[11] Hadeler, K. P. and Glas, D. [1983], *Quasimonotone systems and convergence to equilibrium in a population genetic model*, J. Math. Anal. Appl. **95**, 297–303.

[12] Hirsch, M. W. [1995], *Fixed points of monotone maps*, J. Diff. Equations, 171-179.

[13] Hirsch, M. W. [1985], *Attractors for discrete-time monotone dynamical systems in strongly ordered spaces*, in Geometry and Topology (J. Alexander and J. Harer, eds.), Lecture Notes in Mathematics **1167**, pages 141–153, New York. Proceedings of Special Year at University of Maryland, Springer-Verlag.

[14] Hirsch, M. W. [1985], *Systems of differential equations that are competitive or cooperative II: Convergence almost everywhere*, SIAM J. Math. Anal. **16**, 432–439.

[15] Hirsch, M. W. [1988], *Stability and convergence in strongly monotone dynamical systems*, J. reine angewandte Math. **383**, 1–53.

[16] Hirsch, M. W. [1993], *Asymptotic phase, shadowing and reaction diffusion systems*, in Control Theory, Dynamical Systems and Geometry of Dynamics (K. D. Elworthy, W. N. Everitt and E. B. Lee, eds.), Chapter: Asymptotic phase, shadowing and reaction diffusion systems, pages 87–99. Marcel Dekker, New York. Proceedings of a festschrift in honor of Lawrence Markus.

[17] Hirsch, M. W. and Smale, S. [1974], *Differential Equations, Dynamical Systems, and Linear Algebra*, Academic Press, New York.

[18] Kushner, H. J. and Clark, D. S. [1978], *Stochastic Approximation Methods for Constrained and Unconstrained Systems*, Springer, Berlin, Heidelberg, New York.

[19] Noble, B. and Daniel, J. [1988], *Applied Linear Algebra*, Prentice Hall, Englewood Cliffs, NJ.

[20] Takáč, P. [1991], *Domains of attraction of generic ω-limit sets for strongly monotone semiflows*, Zeits. Analysis **3**, 275–317.

[21] Pemantle, R. [1990], *Nonconvergence to unstable points in urn models and stochastic approximations*, Annals of Probability **18**, 698–712.

[22] Poincaré, H. [1892, 1893, 1899], *Les Méthodes Nouvelles de la Mécanique Céleste*, volume 1,2,3. Gauthiers-Villars, Paris.

[23] Polàčik, P. [1989], *Convergence in smooth strongly monotone flows defined by semilinear parabolic equations*, J. Diff. Equations **79**, 89–110.

[24] Pugh, C. C. and Robinson, C. [1983], *The C^1 closing lemma*, Ergodic Th. Dyn. Sys. **3**, 261–313.

[25] Robinson, J. [1951], *An iterative method for solving a game*, Annals of Mathematics **54**, 296–301.

[26] Smale, S. [1976], *On the differential equations of species in competition*, J. Math. Biology **3**, 5–7.

[27] Smith, H. L. and Thieme, H. [1991], *Convergence for strongly order-preserving semiflows*, SIAM J. Math. Anal. **22**, 1081–1101.

[28] Topkis, D. M. [1979], *Equilibrium points in non-zero sum n-person submodular games*, SIAM J. Control and Optimization **17(6)**, 773–787.

[29] Vives, X. [1990], *Nash equilibrium with strategic complementariies*, J. Math. Econ. **19**, 305–321.

[30] Zhang, W.-B. [1991], *Synergetic Economics*, Springer-Verlag, Berlin and Heidelberg.

Fields Institute Communications
Volume **22**, 1999

A Unified Perspective on Resource Allocation: Limited Arbitrage is Necessary and Sufficient for the Existence of a Competitive Equilibrium, the Core and Social Choice

Graciela Chichilnisky

Director, Program on Information and Resources
and UNESCO Chair in Mathematics and Economics
Columbia University
405 Low Library, 116th and Broadway
New York, NY 10025 USA
gc9@columbia.edu

Abstract. Different forms of resource allocation—by markets, cooperative games, and by social choice—are unified by one condition, *limited arbitrage*, which is defined on the endowments and the preferences of the traders of an Arrow Debreu economy. Limited arbitrage is necessary and sufficient for the existence of a competitive equilibrium in economies with or without short sales, and with finitely or infinitely many markets. The same condition is also necessary and sufficient for the existence of the core, for resolving Arrow's paradox on choices of large utility values, and for the existence of social choice rules which are continuous, anonymous and respect unanimity, thus providing a unified perspective on standard procedures for resource allocation. When limited arbitrage does not hold, *social diversity* of various degrees is defined by the properties of a topological invariant of the economy, the cohomology rings CH of a family of cones which are naturally associated with it. CH has additional information about the resource allocation properties of subsets of traders in the economy and of the subeconomies which they span.

1991 *Mathematics Subject Classification.* 62Cxx.

The paper was an invited presentation at the International Economics Association Round Table on Social Choice, Schloss Hernstein, Vienna, Austria, May, 1994. Research support was provided by NSF Grants SBR 92-16028 and DMS 94-08798, and by the Sloan Foundation Project on Information Technology and Productivity.

The main results of this paper appeared in "Markets, Arbitrage and Social Choice", paper presented at the October 12, 1991, conference "Columbia Celebrates Arrow's Contributions", Columbia University, New York. Editorial comments and intellectual input from Kenneth Arrow, Walt Heller, Ted Groves, Morris Hirsch and Wayne Shafer are gratefully acknowledged.

Introduction

Social diversity is central to resource allocation. People trade because they are different. Gains from trade and the scope for mutually advantageous reallocation depend naturally on the diversity of the traders' preferences and endowments. The market owes its existence to the diversity of those who make up the economy.

An excess of diversity could however stretch the ability of economic institutions to operate efficiently. This is a concern in regions experiencing extensive and rapid migration, such as Canada, the USA and the ex-USSR. Are there natural limits on the degree of social diversity with which existing institutions can cope? This paper will argue that there are. I will argue that not only is a certain amount of diversity essential for the functioning of markets, but, at the other extreme, that too much diversity of a society's preferences and endowments may hinder its ability to allocate resources efficiently.

Somewhat unexpectedly, the very same level of diversity which hinders the functioning of markets also hinders the functioning of democracy, and other forms of resource allocation which are obtained through cooperative games, such as the core.[1] The main tenet of this paper is that there is a crucial level of social diversity which determines whether all these forms of resource allocation will function properly.

Social diversity has been an elusive concept until recently. I give here a precise definition, and examine its impact on the most frequently used forms of resource allocation. From this analysis a new unified perspective emerges: a well-defined connection between resource allocation by markets, games and social choices, which have been considered distinct until now. I define a limitation on social diversity which links all these forms of resource allocation. This limitation is a condition on the endowments and the preferences of the traders of an Arrow Debreu economy. In its simpler form I call this **limited arbitrage**[2]. This concept is related with that of "no-arbitrage"[3] used in finance, but it is nonetheless different from it. I show that limited arbitrage is necessary and sufficient for the existence of an equilibrium in Arrow Debreu economies, and this equivalence extends to economies with or without short sales[4] and with finitely or infinitely many markets,[5] Theorems 2 and 5. Limited arbitrage is also necessary and sufficient for the existence of the core,[6] Theorem 7, and its simplest failure is sufficient for the existence of the **supercore**, a concept which is introduced to gauge social cohesion, Theorem 8. In addition, limited arbitrage is necessary and sufficient for solving Arrow's paradox [1] on choices of large utility value, i.e., for the existence of well-defined social choice rules,[7] Theorem 9. It is also necessary and sufficient for the existence social choice rules which are continuous, anonymous and respect unanimity [**7, 9**], Theorem 13. The success of all four forms of resource allocation, by financial and real competitive markets, by cooperative games and by social choice, hinges on precisely the same limitation on the social diversity of the economy.

Shifting the angle of inquiry slightly sheds a different light on the subject. The results predict that a society which allocates resources efficiently by markets, collective choices or cooperative games, must exhibit no more than a certain degree of social diversity. This is an implicit prediction about the characteristics of those societies which implement successfully these forms of resource allocation. Increases in social diversity beyond this threshold may call for forms of resource allocation which are different from all those which are used today.

The results of this paper are intuitively clear. New forms of resource allocation appear to be needed in order to organize effectively a diverse society. But the issue is largely avoided by thinkers and policy makers alike because the institutions required for this do not yet exist, creating an uncomfortable vacuum. This paper attempts to formalize the problem within a rigorous framework and so provide a solid basis for theory and policy.

As defined here *social diversity* comes in many "shades", of which limited arbitrage is only one. The whole concept of social diversity is subtle and complex. It is encapsuled in an algebraic object, a family of cohomology rings[8] denoted CH, which are naturally associated with a family of cones defined from the endowments and preferences of the traders in the economy. Limited arbitrage simply measures whether the cones intersect or not, while the rings CH measure this and more: CH reveal the intricate topology of how these cones are situated with respect to each other. The cohomology rings CH give a **topological invariant** of the economy, in the sense that CH is invariant under continuous deformations of the measurement of commodities. It is also structurally stable, remaining invariant under small errors of measurement. This concept of diversity is therefore ideal for the social sciences where measurements are imprecise and difficult to obtain. The properties of CH predict specific properties of the economy such as which subeconomies have a competitive equilibrium and which do not, which have a social choice rule and which do not, which have a core, and which have a supercore, Theorem 8. The latter concept, the supercore, measures the extent of social cohesion, namely the extent to which a society has reasons to stay together or break apart. I prove that, somewhat paradoxically, the mildest form of social diversity predicts whether the supercore exists, even in economies where the preferences may not be convex.

The results presented here have two distinguishing features. One is that they provide a minimal condition which ensures that an Arrow Debreu equilibrium,[9] the core and social choice rules exist, namely a condition which is simultaneously necessary and sufficient for the existence of solutions to each of these three forms of resource allocation. The second is they extend and unify the Arrow Debreu formulation of markets to encompass economies with or without short sales[10] and with finitely or infinitely many markets.

While sufficient conditions for the existence of a competitive equilibrium have been known for about forty years, starting from the works of Von Neumann, Nash, Arrow and Debreu, the study of necessary and sufficient for resource allocation introduced in ([**11, 13, 17, 18, 19, 22, 23**]) had been neglected previously. A necessary and sufficient condition is a useful tool. As an illustration consider the necessary and sufficient ("first order") conditions for partial equilibrium analysis of convex problems. These are among the most widely used tools in economics: they identify and help compute solutions in the theories of the consumer and of the firm, and in optimal growth theory. Equally useful could be a necessary and sufficient condition for the existence of market clearing allocations. Furthermore, in order to prove the equivalence between different problems of resource allocation one needs "tight" characterizations: a necessary and sufficient condition for equilibrium, the core and social choice is needed to establish the equivalence of these different forms of resource allocation.

It seems useful to elaborate on a geometric interpretation of limited arbitrage because it clarifies its fundamental links with the problem of resource allocation. It was recently established that the non-empty intersection of the cones which defines

limited arbitrage is equivalent to a topological condition on the spaces of preferences [8, 17]. The topological condition is **contractibility**, a form of similarity of
preferences[11] [7, 36]). Contractibility is necessary and sufficient for the existence
of social choice rules, see [27]. It turns out that the equivalence between non-empty
intersection and contractibility is the link between markets and social choices. The
contractibility of the space of preferences is necessary and sufficient for the existence
of social choice rules, while non-empty intersection (limited arbitrage) is necessary
and sufficient for the existence of a market equilibrium. A recent result brings all
this together: *a family of convex sets has a non-empty intersection if and only if
every subfamily has a contractible union*, see [8, 17].[12]

Using similar topological results,[13] Theorem 6 establishes a link between the
number of traders and the number of commodities: it shows the economy has
limited arbitrage if and only if every subeconomy of $N + 1$ traders does, where N
is the number of commodities traded in the market.

As already mentioned, I consider economies with or without short sales: net
trades are either bounded below, as in a standard Arrow Debreu economy, or they
are not bounded at all. This is a considerable extension from the Arrow Debreu
theory, as it includes financial markets in which short trades typically occur.[14] In
addition, the economy could have finitely or infinitely many markets: the results
obtained in either case[15], Theorem 3.

It is somewhat surprising that the same condition of limited arbitrage is necessary and sufficient for the existence of a market equilibrium with or without short
sales (Theorem 2).[16] The non-existence of a competitive equilibrium is seemingly a
different phenomenon in economies with short sales than it is in economies without
short sales. With short sales, the problem of non-existence arises when traders with
very different preferences[17] desire to take unboundedly large positions against each
other, positions which cannot be accommodated within a bounded economy. Instead, without short sales, the problem arises when some traders have zero income.
Yet I show that in both cases the source of the problem is the same: the diversity
of the traders leads to ill-defined demand behavior at the potential market clearing
prices, and prevents the existence of a competitive equilibrium. Limited arbitrage
ensures that none of these problems arise: with or without short sales it bounds
the diversity of traders precisely as needed for a competitive equilibrium to exist.
Theorem 3 links the number of markets with the number of traders in a somewhat
unexpected manner.

It is somewhat surprising that the same condition of limited arbitrage ensures
the existence of an equilibrium in economies with either finitely or infinitely many
markets. The problem of existence appears to be different in these two cases, and
indeed they are treated quite differently in the literature. A typical problem in
economies with infinitely many markets is that positive orthants have empty interior, so that a standard tool, the Hahn-Banach theorem, cannot be used to find
equilibrium prices for efficient allocations.[18] A solution to this problem was found
in 1980: in [26], extended the Hahn-Banach theorem by introducing a **cone condition** and proving that it is necessary and sufficient for supporting convex sets
whether or not they have an interior. Thereafter the cone condition has been used
extensively to prove existence in economies with infinitely many markets and is
by now a standard condition on preferences defined on infinitely many markets,
known also under the name of "properness" of preferences in subsequent work.[19]
The fundamental new fact presented here is that limited arbitrage implies the cone
condition on efficient and affordable allocations, Theorem 3.[20] Therefore by itself

limited arbitrage provides a unified treatment of economies with finitely and infinitely many markets, being necessary and sufficient for the existence of equilibrium and the core in all cases.

In a nutshell: in all cases limited arbitrage bounds gains from trade, Proposition 4, and is equivalent to the compactness of the set of Pareto efficient utility allocations, Theorem 1.[21] Gains from trade and the Pareto frontier are fundamental concepts involved in most forms of resource allocation: in markets, in games and in social choice. Limited arbitrage controls them all.

1 Definitions and Examples

An Arrow Debreu market $E = \{X, \Omega_h, u_h, h = 1, ..., H\}$ has $H \geq 2$ traders, indexed $h = 1, ..., H$, $N \geq 2$ commodities and consumption or trading space[22] $X = R^N_+$ or $X = R^N$; in Section 5, X is a Hilbert space of infinite dimension. The vector $\Omega_h \in R^N_+$ denotes trader h's property rights or initial endowment and $\Omega = (\sum_{h=1}^{H} \Omega_h)$ is the total endowment of the economy; when $X = R^N_+$, $\Omega >> 0$.[23] Traders may have zero endowments of some goods. Each trader h has a continuous and convex preference represented by $u_h : X \to R$. This paper treats in a unified way general convex preferences whose normalized gradients define either an open or a closed map on every indifference surface so that either (i) all indifference surfaces contain no half lines or (ii) the normalized gradients to any closed set of indifferent vectors define a closed set. Some traders may have preferences of one type, and some of the other. Case (i) includes strictly convex preferences, and case (ii) linear preferences. All the assumptions and the results in this paper are ordinal;[24] therefore without loss of generality one considers utilities representations so that for all h, $u_h(0) = 0$ and $\sup_{\{x:x \in X\}} u_h(x) = \infty$. Preferences are increasing, i.e., $x > y \Rightarrow u_h(x) \geq u_h(y)$. When $X = R^N_+$ either indifference surfaces of positive utility are contained in the interior of X, R^N_{++}, such as Cobb-Douglas utilities, or if an indifference surface of positive utility intersects a boundary ray, it does so transversally.[25]

Definition 1 *A preference is* **uniformly non-satiated** *when it is represented by a utility u_h with a bounded rate of increase,[26] e.g., for smooth preferences:* $\exists \varepsilon, K > 0 : \forall x \in X, K > \|Du_h(x)\| > \varepsilon$.

Uniformly non-satiated preferences are rather common: for example, preferences represented by linear utilities are uniformly non-satiated. The condition is a generalization of a standard Liftschitz condition.

Proposition 1 *If a utility function $u_h : R^N \to R$ is uniformly non-satiated its indifference surfaces are within uniform distance from each other, i.e. $\forall r, s \in R, \exists N(r, s) \in R$ such that $x \in u_h^{-1}(r) \Rightarrow \exists y \in u_h^{-1}(s)$ with $\|x - y\| \leq N(r, s)$.*

Proof This is immediate from the definition. $\square$

The preference in Figure 1 is not uniformly nonsatiated.

> **Assumption 1. When $X = R^N$, the preferences in the economy E are uniformly non-satiated.**

This includes preferences which are strictly convex or not, preferences whose indifference surfaces of positive utility intersect the boundary or not, and preferences whose indifference surfaces contain half lines or not, and are bounded below or not. Figure 2 illustrates.

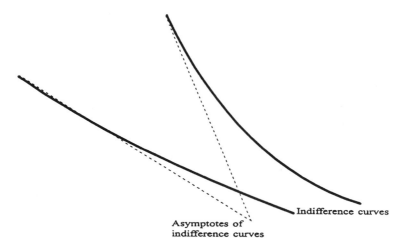

Figure 1 This preference is not uniformly nonsatiated because two indifference surfaces spread apart forever.

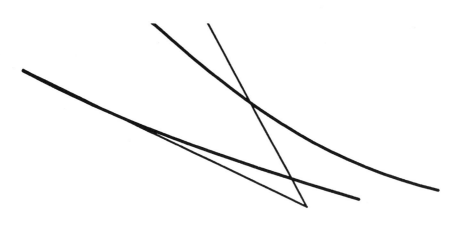

Figure 2 This preference is uniformly nonsatiated

The space of **feasible allocations** is $\Upsilon = \{(x_1, ..., x_H) \in X^H : \sum_{h=1}^{H} x_h = \Omega\}$. The set of **supports to individually rational affordable efficient resource allocations** is:

$$S(\mathsf{E}) = \{v \in R^N : \text{ if } (x_1...x_H) \in \Upsilon \text{ with } u_h(x_h) \geq u_h(\Omega_h) \forall h = 1, ...H,$$

$$\langle v, x_h - \Omega_h \rangle = 0, \text{ then } u_h(z_h) \geq u_h(x_h) \; \forall h \text{ implies } \langle v, z_h - x_h \rangle \geq 0\}.$$

$$(1)$$

The set of **prices orthogonal to the endowments** is[27]

$$N = \{v \in R_+^N - \{0\} : \exists h \text{ with } \langle v, \Omega_h \rangle = 0\}. \tag{2}$$

The **utility possibility set** of the economy E is the set of feasible and individually rational utility allocations:

$$U(E) = \{(V_1, ..., V_H) : \forall h, V_h = u_h(x_h) \geq u_h(\Omega_h) \geq 0, \text{ for some } (x_1, ..., x_H) \in \Upsilon \}.$$

The **Pareto frontier** of the economy E is the set of feasible, individually rational and efficient utility allocations:

$$P(E) = \{V \in U(E) :\sim \exists W \in U(E) : W > V\} \subset R_+^H. \tag{3}$$

A **competitive equilibrium** of E consists of a price vector $p^* \in R_+^N$ and an allocation $(x_1^*...x_H^*) \in X^H$ such that x_h^* optimizes u_h over the budget set $B_h(p^*) = \{x \in X : \langle x, p^* \rangle = \langle \Omega_h, p^* \rangle\}$ and $\sum_{h=1}^H x_h^* - \Omega_h = 0$.

1.1 Global and Market Cones. Two cases, $X = R^N$ and $X = R_+^N$, are considered separately.

- **Consider first** $X = R^N$.

Definition 2 *For trader h define the cone of directions along which utility increases without bound:*

$$A_h(\Omega_h) = \{x \in X : \forall y \in X, \exists \lambda > 0 : u_h(\Omega_h + \lambda x) > u_h(y)\}.$$

This cone contains global information on the economy and is new in the literature.[28] In ordinal terms, the rays of this cone intersect all indifference surfaces corresponding to bundles preferred by u_h to Ω_h. We now introduce another cone: the cone A_h and the part of its boundary along which utility never ceases to increase define a **global cone**

$$G_h(\Omega_h) = \{x \in X \text{ and } \sim \exists Max_{\lambda \geq 0} u_h(\Omega_h + \lambda x)\}.$$

This cone treats all convex preferences in a unified way and under Assumption 1 it has a simple structure: when preferences have half lines in their indifferences $G_h(\Omega_h)$ equals $A_h(\Omega_h)$; when indifferences contain no half lines, then $G_h(\Omega_h)$ is its closure: it is therefore new in the literature and identical to the global cone introduced in [**22**], [29] see [**24**], Appendix.

Definition 3 *The* **market cone** *of trader h is*

$$D_h(\Omega_h) = \{z \in X : \forall y \in G_h(\Omega_h), \langle z, y \rangle > 0\}. \tag{4}$$

D_h is the cone of prices assigning strictly positive value to all directions of net trades leading to eventually increasing utility. This is a convex cone.

The following proposition establishes the structure of the global cones, and is used in proving the connection between limited arbitrage, equilibrium and the core:

Proposition 2 *If the function $u_h : R^N \to R$ is uniformly non-satiated, the sets :*

$B_h(\omega_h) = \{z \in X : \forall \lambda > 0, u_h(\omega_h + \lambda z) \neq \lim_{\lambda \to \infty} u_h(\omega_h + \lambda z) < \infty$ *and u_h increases with $\lambda\}$,*

$C_h(\omega_h) = \{z \in X : \exists N : \lambda, \mu > N \Rightarrow u_h(\omega_h + \lambda z) = u_h(\omega_h + \mu)$ *and u_h increases with $\lambda\}$, and the global cone $G_h(\omega_h)$ are all uniform across all vectors in the space, and,*

For general non-satiated preferences $G_h(\omega_h)$ and $B_h(\omega_h)$ may not be uniform.

Under Assumption 2: (i) The cone $G_h(\Omega_h)$ equals $A_h(\Omega_h)$ when indifferences contain half lines (case (ii)) and its closure when they do not, (case (i)), and thus it is identical to the global cone defined in [22].

Proof See also Chichilnisky [22] and [25], p. 461. The three sets $A_h(\omega_h)$, $B_h(\omega_h)$ and $C_h(\omega_h)$ are disjoint pairwise and

$$A_h(\omega_h) \cup B_h(\omega_h) \cup C_h(\omega_h) \cup H_h(\omega_h) = R^N. \tag{5}$$

where $H_h(\omega_h)$ is the complement of $A_h(\omega_h) \cup B_h(\omega_h) \cup C_h(\omega_h)$, i.e., the set of directions along which the utility achieves a maximum value and decreases thereafter.

The first step is to show that $B_h(\Omega_h) \cup C_h(\Omega_h) \subset \partial A_h(\Omega_h)$. Observe that monotonicity and the condition of uniform nonsatiation imply that the rate of increase is uniformly bounded below along the direction defined by the vector $(1, ..., 1)$ (or along any direction defined by a strictly positive vector). This implies that if $z \in B_h(\Omega_h) \cup C_h(\Omega_h)$

$$s >> z \Rightarrow s \in A_h(\Omega_h)$$

and

$$s << z \Rightarrow s \in H_h(\Omega_h).$$

Therefore the set $B_h(\Omega_h) \cup C_h(\Omega_h)$ is in the boundary of the set $A_h(\Omega_h)$. The relation between $G_h(\Omega_h)$ and $A_h(\Omega_h)$ is now immediate, cf., [22], p. 85, (4) and [24], Appendix.

The next step is to show that $A_h(\Omega_h)$ is identical everywhere. It suffices to show that if two different half-lines $l = \{\Omega_h + \lambda v\}_{\lambda \geq 0}$ and $m = \{\Lambda_h + \lambda v\}_{\lambda \geq 0}$ are parallel translates of each other, and $l \subset A_h(\Omega_h)$, then $m \subset A_h(\Lambda_h), \forall \Lambda_h \in m$. This is immediate from Assumption 1, which ensures that the rate of increase of the function u_h is bounded above: if the values of the function u_h on m were bounded above, while exceeding every bounded value over the (parallel) line l, then the rate of increase of the utility would be unbounded above.

By assumption, preferences either have half lines in their indifferences, or they don't: in either case the sets $B_h(\Omega_h)$ and $C_h(\Omega_h)$ are uniform. In addition, $A_h(\Omega_h)$ is uniform as well. Therefore to complete the proof it remains only to show that the cones $G_h(\Omega_h)$ are the same everywhere under Assumption 1.

Observe that for a general convex preference represented by a utility u_h the set $G_h(\Omega_h)$ may vary as the vector Ω_h varies, since the set $B_h(\Omega_h)$ itself may vary with Ω_h: at some Ω_h a direction $z \in \partial G_h$ may be in $B_h(\Omega_h)$ and at others $B_h(\Omega_h)$ may be empty and $z \in C_h(\Omega_h)$ instead. This occurs when along a ray defined by a vector z from one endowment the utility levels asymptote to a finite limit but do not reach their limiting value, while at other endowments, along the same direction z, they achieve this limit. This example, and a similar reasoning for $A_h(\Omega_h)$, proves (iv). However, such cases are excluded here, since under our assumptions on preferences, for each trader, either all indifference surfaces contain half lines, or none do. This completes the proof of the proposition. □

- **Consider next the case:** $X = R^N_+$

Definition 4 *The* **market cone of trader** h *is:*

$$D_h^+(\Omega_h) = D_h(\Omega_h) \bigcap S(\mathsf{E}) \ \ if \ S(\mathsf{E}) \subset \mathsf{N},$$

$$= D_h(\Omega_h) \ otherwise. \tag{6}$$

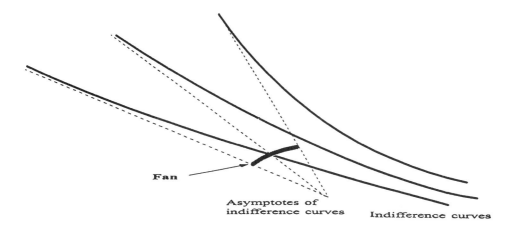

Figure 3 This preference has a 'fan' of different directions along which the utility values reach a bounded utility value. Assumption 1 is not satisfied. All the directions in the fan are in the recession cone but not in the global cone G_h nor in the cone A_h.

where $S(\mathsf{E})$ and N are defined in (1) and (2).[30]

There is no analog to Proposition 2 when $X = R_+^N$; indeed, when $X = R_+^N$ the market cones $D_h^+(\Omega_h)$ typically vary with the initial endowments. However, when $\Omega_h \in R_{++}^N$, the interior of R_+^N, then $D_h^+(\Omega_h) = D_h(\Omega_h)$ and therefore $D_h^+(\Omega_h)$ is the same for all endowments in R_{++}^N.

Proposition 3 *When $X = R_+^N$ and an indifference surface of u_h corresponding to a positive consumption bundle $x > 0$ intersects a boundary ray*[31] $r \subset \partial X$, *then $r \in G_h(0)$.*[32]

Proof Recall that we assumed $u_h(0) = 0$, and that the preference's indifference surfaces of positive utility are either (a) contained in the interior of R_+^N, R_{++}^N, or (b) they intersect a boundary ray r of R_+^N and do so transversally. In case (a) the proposition is satisfied trivially, because no indifference surface of strictly positive value ever intersects the boundary of R_+^N. In case (b) the proposition follows immediately from the definition of transversality. Observe that it is possible that $sup_{x \in r}(u_h(x)) < \infty$. $\square$

1.2 The Core and the Supercore.

Definition 5 *The **core** of the economy E is the set of allocations which no coalition can improve upon within its own endowments:*

$$C(\mathsf{E}) = \{(x_1, ..., x_H) \in R^{N \times H} : \sum_h (x_h - \Omega_h) = 0 \text{ and } \sim J \subset \{1, ..., H\} :$$

$$\text{and } \{y_h\}_{h \in J} \ s.t. \sum_{j \in J} (y_j - \Omega_j) = 0, \forall j \in J, u_j(y_j) \geq u_j(x_j),$$

$$\text{and } \exists j \in J : u_j(y_j) > u_j(x_j)\}.$$

Definition 6 *The **supercore** of the economy is the set of allocations which no **strict** subcoalition can improve using only its own endowments. It is therefore a superset of the core:*

$$SC(\mathsf{E}) = \{\{(x_1, ..., x_H) \in R^{N \times H} : \sum_h (x_h - \Omega_h) = 0 \text{ and } \sim J \subset \{1, ..., \}] :$$

$$J \neq \{1, ..., H\} \text{ and } \{y_h\}_{h \in J} \text{ s.t. } \forall j \in J, u_j(y_j) \geq u_j(x_j), \sum_{j \in J}(y_j - \Omega_j) = 0,$$

$$\text{and } \exists j \in J : u_j(y_j) > u_j(x_j)\}.$$

By construction, $C(\mathsf{E}) \subset SC(\mathsf{E})$. The motivation for this concept is as follows: if an allocation is in the supercore, no strict subcoalition of traders can improve upon this by itself. A non-empty supercore means that no strict subsets of individuals can do better than by joining the entire group. The benefits from joining the larger group exceed those available to any subgroup. One can say therefore that an economy with a non-empty supercore has reasons to stay together: There is no reason for such a society to break apart. If an economy has stayed together for some time, it probably has a non-empty supercore.

2 Limited arbitrage: definition and examples

This section provides the definition of limited arbitrage. It gives an intuitive interpretation for limited arbitrage in terms of gains from trade, and contrasts limited arbitrage with the arbitrage concept used in financial markets. It provides examples of economies with and without limited arbitrage.

Definition 7 *When $X = R^N$, E satisfies **limited arbitrage** when*

$$(LA) \quad \bigcap_{h=1}^{H} D_h \neq \emptyset.$$

Definition 8 *When $X = R_+^N$, E satisfies **limited arbitrage** when*

$$(LA^+) \quad \bigcap_{h=1}^{H} D_h^+(\Omega_h) \neq \emptyset. \tag{7}$$

2.1 Interpretation of Limited Arbitrage as Bounded Gains From Trade when $X = R^N$. Limited arbitrage has a simple interpretation in terms of gains from trade when $X = R^N$. Gains from trade are defined by:

$$\mathsf{G}(\mathsf{E}) = \sup \left\{ \sum_{h=1}^{H}(u_h(x_h) - u_h(\Omega_h)) \right\}, \text{ where}$$

$$\sum_{h=1}^{H}(x_h - \Omega_h) = 0, \text{ and } \forall h, \ u_h(x_h) \geq u_h(\Omega_h) \geq 0.$$

The Proposition below applies to preferences where the normalized gradients define a closed map on every indifference surface, i.e., case (ii); the Corollary following it applies both to case (i) and (ii):

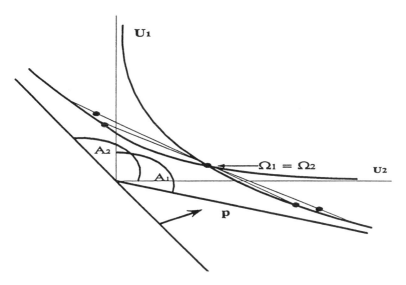

Figure 4 Limited arbitrage is satisfied: feasible allocations lead to bounded utility increases.

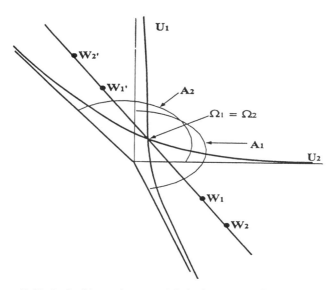

Figure 5 Limited arbitrage is not satisfied: there exist a feasible unbounded sequence of allocations, $(W_1, W_1'), (W_2, W_2'), ...$, along which both traders' utility never ceases to increase.

Proposition 4 *In case (ii), the economy* E *satisfies limited arbitrage if and only if gains from trade are bounded,*[33] *i.e., if and only if*

$$\mathsf{G}(\mathsf{E}) < \infty.$$

Proof See also Chichilnisky [**22**] and [**24**]. Assume E has limited arbitrage. If $\mathsf{G}(\mathsf{E})$ was not bounded there would exist a sequence of net trades $(z_1^j...z_H^j)_{j=1,2...}$ such that

(i) $\forall j$, $\sum_{h=1}^{H} z_h^j = 0$, $\forall h, j$ $u_h(z_h^j) \geq 0$, and

(ii) for some $h = g$, $\lim_{j \to \infty}(u_g(\Omega_g + z_g^j)) \to \infty$.

Next I show that if $\|z_h^j\| \to \infty$, and $\{z_h^j/\|z_h^j\|\}_{j=1,2,...}$ denotes a convergent subsequence, then $z_h = \lim_j z_h^j/\|z_h^j\| \in \overline{G}_h$. The proof is by contradiction. By Proposition 2 the cone $\overline{G}_h$ is uniform so without loss of generality we may assume that $\forall h$ $\Omega_h = 0$. If $z_h \in \overline{G}_h^c,$[34] then by quasiconcavity of u_h and by Proposition 2, along the ray defined by z_h the utility u_h achieves a maximum level u^o, say at $\lambda_o z$, for some $\lambda_o \geq 0$, and it decreases thereafter, i.e., $\lambda > \lambda_o \Rightarrow u_h(\lambda z) < u^o$. Define a function $\theta : R_+ \to R_+$ by $u_h(\lambda z_h + \theta(\lambda)e) = u^o$, where $e = (1, ..., 1)$. I will show that θ is a convex function so necessarily $\lim_{\lambda \to \infty}\theta(\lambda) = \infty$. By convexity of preferences

$$u^o \leq u_h(\alpha(\lambda z_h + \theta(\lambda)e) + (1 - \alpha)(\lambda' z_h + \theta(\lambda')e)$$

$$= u_h((\alpha\lambda + (1 - \alpha)\lambda')z_h + (\alpha\theta(\lambda) + (1 - \alpha)(\theta(\lambda'))e).$$

Thus by monotonicity and by the definition of the map θ, $\theta(\alpha\lambda + (1 - \alpha)\lambda') \leq \alpha\theta(\lambda) + (1 - \alpha)\theta(\lambda')$, which proves convexity. So necessarily $\lim_{\lambda \to \infty}\theta(\lambda) = \infty$.

Assumption 1 together with monotonicity implies that the rate of increase of u_h along the direction defined by e (or by any strictly positive vector) is uniformly bounded below: $\exists \varepsilon > 0 :| u_h(x + \theta e) - u_h(x) |\geq \theta.\varepsilon, \forall \theta \in R_+, \forall x \in R^N$. Therefore $u_h(\lambda z_h + \theta(\lambda)e) \equiv u^o \geq u_h(\lambda z_h) + \theta(\lambda)\varepsilon$, so that $u_h(\lambda z_h) \leq u^o - \theta(\lambda)e$. Note that $\theta(\lambda_o) = 0$ and $\theta(\lambda) > 0$ for $\lambda > \lambda_o$. I showed above that θ is a convex function. Therefore $\lim_{\lambda \to \infty}\theta(\lambda) = \infty$; since $u_h(\lambda z_h) \leq u^o - \theta(\lambda)e$ then $\lim_{\lambda \to \infty}u_h(\lambda z_h) = -\infty$. It follows that $z_h \in \overline{G}_h$ for otherwise as we have seen $\lim_{j \to \infty}u_h(z_h^j) < 0$ contradicting the fact that the utility levels of $(z_1^j, ..., z_H^j)_{j=1,2...}$ are positive.

Recall that for some $g, \lim_{j \to \infty}u_g(z_g^j) \to \infty$. By Assumption 1, $\exists K > 0 :| u_g(x) - u_g(y) |\leq K \| x - y \| \forall x, y \in R^N$, so that for any n and $j \mid u_g(z_g^n) - u_g(z_g^n - je) |\leq K \| je \|$. Since $u_g (z_g^j) \to \infty$, for every j there exists an n_j such that $u_g(z_g^{n_j} - je) > j$. Take the sequence $\{z_g^{n_j}\}$ and relabel it $\{z_g^j\}$. Now consider the new sequence of allocations $\{z_1^j + \frac{je}{H-1}, ..., z_g^j - je, ..., z_H^j + \frac{je}{H-1}\}$ and call it also $\{z_h^j\}_{h=1,2,...,H}$. For each j this defines a feasible allocation and, by Assumption 1, along this sequence $\forall h$, $u_h(z_h^j) \to \infty$. In particular $\forall h, \| z_h^j \|\to \theta$.

Define now C as the set of all strictly positive convex combinations of the vectors $z_h = \lim_j z_h^j/\|z_h^j\|$ for all h. Then either C is strictly contained in a half space, or it defines a subspace of R^N. Since $\sum_{h=1}^{H} z_h^j = 0$, C cannot be strictly contained in a half space. Therefore C defines a subspace. In particular for any given $g, \exists \lambda_h \geq 0 \ \forall h$ such that $(*) - z_g = \sum_{h=1}^{H} \lambda_h z_h$. If one trader had indifference surfaces without half lines (case (i)) then $G_g = \overline{G}_g$ and $z_g \in \overline{G}_g \Rightarrow z_g \in G_g$, so that limited arbitrage would contradict $(*)$, because there can be no p such that $\langle p, x \rangle > 0$ for $x \in \overline{G}_h$ and $\langle p, x \rangle > 0$ for $x \in G_g$. When instead for every closed sequence of indifferent vectors the corresponding normals define a closed set, i.e., all preferences are in case (ii), then the global cone G_h is open [22] so that G_h^c is a closed set, and the set of directions in G_h^c is compact. On each direction of G_h^c the utility u_h achieves a maximum by definition; therefore under the conditions on preferences there exists a maximum utility level for u_h over all directions in G_h^c. Since along the sequence $\{z_h^j\}$ every trader's utility increases without bound, $\forall h \exists j_h : j > j_h \Rightarrow z_h^j \in G_h$. However $\sum_{h=1}^{H} z_h^j = 0$, contradicting again limited arbitrage. In all cases the contradiction arises from assuming that $G(E)$ is not bounded, so that $G(E)$ must be bounded. Therefore under Assumption 1, limited arbitrage implies bounded gains from trade. Observe that when all preferences are in case (ii) then $G_h = A_h$. In this case the reciprocal is immediate: limited arbitrage is also necessary for bounded gains from trade, completing the proof. $\qquad\square$

The proof of the sufficiency in Proposition 4 above is valid for all preferences satisfying Assumption 1, case (i) or case (ii), so that:

Corollary 1 *For all economies with uniformly non-satiated preferences, limited arbitrage implies bounded gains from trade.*[33]

2.2 A Financial Interpretation of Limited Arbitrage. It is useful to explain the connection between limited arbitrage and the notion of "no-arbitrage" used in finance. The concepts are generally different, but in certain cases they coincide. In the finance literature, arbitrage appears as a central concept. Financial markets equilibrium is often defined as the absence of market arbitrage. In Walrasian markets this is not the case. It may therefore appear that the two literatures use different equilibrium concepts. Yet the link provided here draws a bridge between these two literatures. As shown below limited arbitrage, while not an equilibrium concept, is necessary and sufficient for the existence of a Walrasian equilibrium. In the following I will show the close link between the two concepts and establish the bridge between the two equilibrium theories. I will provide examples where the two concepts are identical, and others where they are different.

In financial markets an arbitrage opportunity exists when unbounded gains can be made at no cost, or, equivalently, by taking no risks. Consider, for example, buying an asset in a market where its price is low while simultaneously selling it at another where its price is high: this can lead to unbounded gains at no risk to the trader. No-arbitrage means that such opportunities do not exist, and it provides a standard framework for pricing a financial asset: precisely so that no arbitrage opportunities should arise between this and other related assets. Since trading does not cease until all arbitrage opportunities are extinguished, at a market clearing equilibrium there must be no-arbitrage.

The simplest illustration of the link between limited arbitrage and no-arbitrage is an economy E where the traders' initial endowments are zero, $\Omega_h = 0$ for $h = 1, 2$, and the set of gradients to indifference surfaces are closed. Here no-arbitrage at the initial endowments means that there are no trades which could increase the traders' utilities at zero cost: gains from trade in E must be zero. By contrast, E has limited arbitrage when no trader can increase utility beyond a given bound at zero cost; as seen above, gains from trade are bounded.

In brief: *no-arbitrage* requires that there should be no gains from trade at zero cost while *limited arbitrage* requires that there should be only bounded utility arbitrage or limited gains from trade.

Now consider a particular case of the same example: when the traders' utilities are defined by linear real valued functions. Then the two concepts coincide: there is limited arbitrage if and only if there is no-arbitrage as defined in finance. In brief: in linear economies, limited arbitrage "collapses" into no-arbitrage.

In summary, the two concepts are related but nonetheless different: no-arbitrage is a market clearing condition used to describe an allocation at which there is no further reason to trade. It can be applied at the initial allocations, but then it means that there is no reason for trade in the economy: the economy is autarchic and therefore not very interesting. By contrast, limited arbitrage is applied only to the economy's initial data, the traders' endowments and preferences. Limited arbitrage does not imply that the economy is autarchic; quite to the contrary, it is valuable in predicting whether the economy can ever reach a competitive equilibrium. It allows to do so by examining the economy's initial conditions.

2.3 Examples of markets with and without limited arbitrage.

Example 1 *Figures 4 and 5 above illustrate an economy with two traders trading in $X = R^2$; in Figure 4 the market cones intersect and the economy has limited arbitrage. In Figure 5 the market cones do not intersect and the economy does not have limited arbitrage. Figure 6 below illustrates three traders trading in $X = R^3$; each two market cones intersect, but the three market cones do not intersect, and the economy violates limited arbitrage. This figure illustrates the fact that the union of the market cones may fail to be contractible: indeed, this failure corresponds to the failure of the market cones to intersect, as proven in [17].*

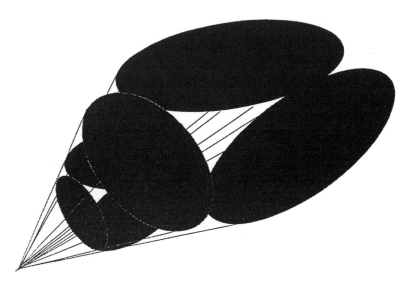

Figure 6 Three traders in R^3. Every two traders's subeconomy has limited arbitrage but the whole economy does not.

Example 2 *When the consumption set is $X = R_+^N$, limited arbitrage is always satisfied if all indifference surfaces through positive consumption bundles are contained in the interior of X, R_{++}^N. Examples of such preferences are those given by Cobb-Douglas utilities, or by utilities with constant elasticity of substitution (CES) with elasticity of substitution $\sigma < 1$. This is because all such preferences have as global cone the positive orthant (or its closure), and therefore their market cones always intersect. These preferences are very similar to each other on choices involving large utility levels: this is a form of similarity of preferences. Economies where the individuals' initial endowments are strictly interior to the consumption set X always satisfy the limited arbitrage condition in the case $X = R_+^N$, since in this case $\forall h$, $R_{++}^N \subset D_h^+(\Omega_h)$ for all $h = 1, ..., H$.*

Example 3 *When $X = R_+^N$ the limited arbitrage condition may fail to be satisfied when some trader's endowment vector Ω_h is in the boundary of the consumption space, ∂R_+^N, and at all supporting prices in $S(\mathsf{E})$ some trader has zero income, i.e.,* when $\forall p \in S(\mathsf{E})\ \exists h$ such that $\langle p, \Omega_h \rangle = 0$. In this case, $S(\mathsf{E}) \subset \mathsf{N}$. This case is illustrated in Figure 7 below; it is a rather general case which may occur in economies with many individuals and with many commodities. When all individuals have positive income at some price $p \in S(\mathsf{E})$, then limited arbitrage is always satisfied since by definition in this case $\forall h, = R_{++}^N \subset D_h^+(\Omega_i)$ for all $h = 1, ..., H$.

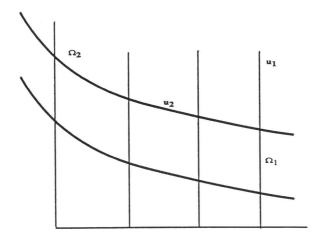

Figure 7 Limited arbitrage fails. Trader two owns only one good, to which the other trader is indifferent.

Example 4 *A competitive equilibrium may exist even when some traders have zero income, showing that Arrow's "resource relatedness" condition [2] is sufficient but not necessary for existence of an equilibrium. Figure 8 below illustrates an economy where at all supporting prices some trader has zero income: $\forall p \in S(\mathsf{E})\ \exists h$ such that $\langle p, \Omega_h \rangle = 0$, i.e., $S(\mathsf{E}) \subset \mathsf{N}$; in this economy, however, limited arbitrage is satisfied so that a competitive equilibrium exists. The initial allocation and a price vector assigning value zero to the second good defines such an equilibrium.*

3 Limited arbitrage and the compactness of the Pareto frontier

The Pareto frontier $P(\mathsf{E})$ is the set of feasible, efficient and individually rational utility allocations. With H traders it is a subset of R_+^H. Proving the boundedness and closedness of the Pareto frontier is a crucial step in establishing the existence of a competitive equilibrium and the non-emptiness of the core. The main theorem of this section shows that limited arbitrage is necessary and sufficient for this.

There is a novel feature of the results which are presented here, a feature which is shared which those that were previously established in [11, 13, 18, 22, 23, 24] and [28, 30]. It starts from the observation that the compactness of the Pareto frontier need not imply the compactness of the set of feasible commodity allocations. The Pareto frontier is defined in *utility* space, R_+^H while the commodity allocations are in the product of the *commodity space* with itself, X^H. When $X = R^N$, the commodity allocations are in $R^{H \times N}$. This observation is useful to distinguish the results presented here, in [11, 13, 18, 22, 23, 24] and [28, 30] from others in

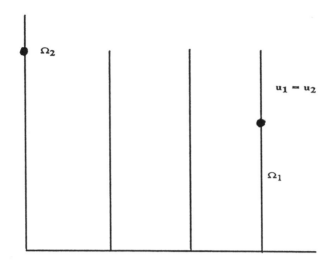

Figure 8 Equilibrium exists even when one trader has zero income

the literature. Other conditions used in the literature which are sufficient for the existence of an equilibrium and the core ensure that—with or without short sales—the set of individually rational and feasible commodity allocations is compact, see, e.g., [29], [46] and [39] among others; the latter proves in detail that Werner's 1987 no-arbitrage condition, based on recession cones, implies the compactness of the set of feasible and individually rational allocations unless preferences are linear. But as already observed, and as is shown below, the boundedness of the set of feasible commodity allocations is *not* needed for existence. Indeed, such boundedness is not used in this paper, nor was it used in the results of Chichilnisky in [11, 13, 18, 19, 20, 22, 24] and [28, 30]: these are the first results in the literature proving the existence of equilibrium and the non-emptiness of the core in economies where limited arbitrage holds and the set of feasible and individually rational allocations is generally unbounded. In addition, of course, these results establish conditions which are simultaneously necessary and sufficient for the existence of equilibrium and the core, another novel feature. As a result, here the set of all possible efficient allocations, the contract curve, and the set of possible equilibria and the set of all possible core allocations, may be unbounded sets. Next we review some examples to illustrate and better appreciate the nature of the problems that can arise.

Example 5 *Figure 9 shows that the Pareto frontier may fail to be closed even in finite dimensional models, provided the consumption set is the whole Euclidean space. It shows two traders with indifference curves having the line $y = -x$ as asymptote. Consumption sets are the whole space and feasible allocations are those which sum to zero. Utility functions are $u_i = x_i + y_i \pm e^{-(x_i - y_i)}, i = 1, 2$. Limited arbitrage rules out such cases.*

Example 6 *Another example is a two-agent economy where both agents have linear preferences: if the preferences are different the set of feasible utility allocations is unbounded. Of course, limited arbitrage rules out such situations.*

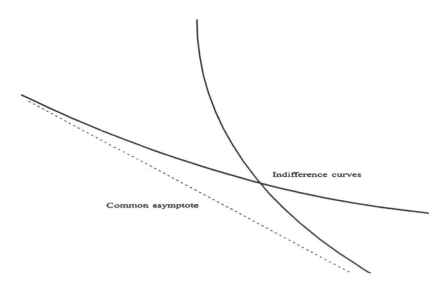

Indifference curves

Common asymptote

Figure 9 The Pareto frontier may fail to be closed even in finite dimensions

Example 7 *Even when the consumption set is bounded below, but the commodity space is infinite dimensional, examples can be provided where the Pareto frontier is not closed.*[35]

Theorem 1 *Consider an economy* E *as defined in Section 1. Then* **limited arbitrage** *is necessary and sufficient for the compactness of the Pareto frontier.*[36]

Proof This result always holds when the consumption set is bounded below by some vector in the space,[37] and in that case it is proved using standard arguments, see, e.g., [**2**]. Therefore in the following I concentrate in the case where X is unbounded.

Sufficiency first. Recall that by definition $P(\mathsf{E}) \subset U(\mathsf{E}) \subset R_+^N$. Proposition 4 and Corollary 1 proved that $U(\mathsf{E})$ is bounded when limited arbitrage is satisfied, so that $P(\mathsf{E})$ is bounded also.

The next step is to prove that $P(\mathsf{E})$ is closed when limited arbitrage is satisfied. Consider a sequence of allocations $\{z_h^j\}_{j=1,2...}$, $h = 1, 2, ..., H$, satisfying $\forall j$, $\sum_{h=1}^H z_h^j \leq \Omega$, and $\lim_{j \to \infty} \sum_{h=1}^H z_h^j = \Omega$. Assume that $(u_1(z_1^j), ..., u_H(z_H^j)) \subset R_+^N$ converges to a utility allocation $v = (v_1, ..., v_H) \in R_+^H$, which is undominated by the utility allocation of any other feasible allocation. Observe that the vector v may or not be the utility vector of a feasible allocation: when limited arbitrage is satisfied, I will prove that it is. The result is immediate if the set of feasible allocations is bounded; therefore I concentrate in the case where the set of feasible allocations is not bounded.

Let M be the set of all traders $h \in \{1, 2., , , H\}$, for whom the corresponding sequence of allocations $\{z_h^j\}_{j=1,2...}$ is bounded, i.e. $h \in M \Leftrightarrow \exists K_h : \|z_h^j\| < K_h < \infty$; let J be its complement, $J = \{1, 2, ..., H\} - M$, which I assume to be non-empty. There exists a subsequence of the original sequence of allocations, which for simplicity is denoted also $\{z_h^j\}_{j=1,2...}$, $h = 1, 2, ..., H$, along which $\forall h \in M$, the $\lim_j \{z_h^j\}_{j=1,2...} = z_h$ exists, and $\sum_{h \in M} z_h + \lim_{j \to \infty} \sum_{h \in J} z_h^j = \Omega$. Recall that by Proposition 2 the cones G_h are uniform, so that we may translate the origin of the space without loss of generality. Therefore we may assume without loss that $\sum_{h \in M} z_h = \Omega$, i.e. that $\lim_{j \to \infty} \sum_{h \in J} z_h^j = 0$. For each $h \in J$, consider the normalized sequence $\{\frac{z_h^j}{\|z_h^j\|}\}_{j=1,2...}$, which is contained in a compact space, the unit ball. A convergent subsequence of this always exists, and is denoted also $\{\frac{z_h^j}{\|z_h^j\|}\}_{j=1,2...}$. Let $z_h = \lim_j \{\frac{z_h^j}{\|z_h^j\|}\}$. We showed in Proposition 4 that, under the conditions, $\forall h \in J, z_h \in \overline{G_h}$. If $\forall h \in J, z_h \notin G_h$ then by Proposition 2 eventually the utility values of the traders attain their limit for all h, the utility vector v is achieved by a feasible allocation and the proof is complete. It remains therefore to consider only the case where for some trader $g \in J, z_g \in G_g$.

Define now the convex cone C of all strictly positive linear combinations of the vectors $\{z_h\}_{h \in J}, C = \{w = \sum_{h \in J} \mu_h z_h, \mu_h > 0\}$. There are two mutually exclusive and exhaustive cases: either (a) the cone C is contained strictly in a half-space of R^N, or (b) the cone C is a subspace of R^N. By construction $\lim_{j \to \infty} \sum_{h \in J} z_h^j = 0$, which eliminates case (a). Therefore (b) must hold, and C is a subspace of R^N. In particular, $-z_g \in C$, i.e., $\forall h \in J \exists \lambda_h \geq 0$ such that

$$-z_g = \sum_{h \in J} \lambda_h z_h. \tag{8}$$

The final step is to show that (8) contradicts limited arbitrage. By limited arbitrage $\exists p \in \cap_h D_h$ s.t. $\langle p, z_g \rangle > 0$, because $z_g \in G_g$, and $\forall h \in J, \langle p, z_h \rangle \geq 0$, since $z_h \in \overline{G_h}$. Therefore $\langle p, \sum_{h \in J} z_h \rangle \geq 0$, which contradicts (8). Since the contradiction arises from assuming that the Pareto frontier $P(\mathsf{E})$ is not closed, $P(\mathsf{E})$ must be closed. Therefore limited arbitrage implies a compact Pareto frontier.

Necessity is established next. If limited arbitrage fails, there is no vector $y \in H$ such that $\langle y, z_h \rangle > 0$ for all $\{z_h\} \in G_h$. Equivalently, there exist a set J consisting of at least two traders and, for each $h \in J$, a vector $z_h \in G_h$ such that $\sum_{h \in J} z_h = 0$. Then by Proposition 2 either for some $h, z_h \in A_h$ so that the Pareto frontier is unbounded and therefore not compact, or else for some $h, z_h \in \partial G_h \cap G_h$ and therefore the Pareto frontier is not closed, and therefore not compact either. In either case, the Pareto frontier is not compact when limited arbitrage fails. Therefore compactness is necessary for limited arbitrage.   □

Proposition 5 *When $X = R^N$, limited arbitrage implies that the Pareto frontier $P(\mathsf{E})$ is homeomorphic to a simplex.*[38]

Proof This follows from Theorem 1 and by the convexity of preferences, cf., [**2**].   □

4 Competitive equilibrium and limited arbitrage

This section establishes the main result linking the existence of a competitive equilibrium with the condition of limited arbitrage.[39] The result is that limited arbitrage is simultaneously necessary and sufficient for the existence of a competitive equilibrium,[40] and it was established for special cases in [**11, 13, 18, 19, 22, 24**]. Other noteworthy features are: the equivalence between limited arbitrage and equilibrium applies equally to economies with or without short sales, and with or without strictly convex preferences. It therefore includes the Arrow Debreu market which has no short sales, a classic case which was neglected previously in the literature on no-arbitrage conditions. In addition, the equivalence applies to economies where the set of feasible and individually rational allocations may be unbounded, a case which has also been neglected in the literature.[41] Finally, the equivalence between limited arbitrage and equilibrium extends to economies with infinitely many markets, see [28, 29] and the next Section.

The result presented below was established first in [11, 13, 19, 22] for uniformly non-satiated convex preferences which are either all in case (i) e.g., strictly convex, or in case (ii), e.g., they have indifference surfaces with a closed set of gradient directions. The result presented here extends these earlier results in that it deals in a unified way with non-satiated convex preferences; in the same economy there may be a mixture of preferences of type (i) and (ii), see also [23, 24]:

Theorem 2 *Consider an economy* $E = \{X, u_h, \Omega_h, h = 1, ..., H\}$, *where* $H \geq 2$, *with* $X = R^N$ *or* $X = R_+^N$ *and* $N \geq 1$. *Then the following two properties are equivalent:*

(i) *The economy* E *has limited arbitrage.*
(ii) *The economy* E *has a competitive equilibrium.*

Proof Necessity first. Consider first the case $X = R^N$ and assume without loss of generality that $\Omega_h = 0$ for all h. The proof is by contradiction. Let p^* be an equilibrium price and let $x^* = (x_1^*, ...x_H^*)$ be the corresponding equilibrium allocation. Then if limited arbitrage does not hold, $\exists h$ and $v \in G_h$ such that $\langle p^*, v \rangle \leq 0$, so that $\forall \lambda > 0$, λv is affordable at prices p^*. However, G_h is the same at any endowment by Proposition 2. It follows that $\exists \lambda > 0 : u_h(x_h^* + \lambda v) > u_h(x_h^*)$, which contradicts the fact that x_h^* is an equilibrium allocation. This completes the proof of necessity when $X = R^N$.

Consider next $X = R_+^N$. Assume that $\forall q \in S(E)$ $\exists h \in \{1, ..., H\}$ such that $\langle q, \Omega_h \rangle = 0$. Then if limited arbitrage is not satisfied $\bigcap_{h=1}^H D_h^+(\Omega_h) = \emptyset$, which implies that $\forall p \in R^N$, $\exists h$ and $v(p) \in G_h(\Omega_h)$:

$$\langle p, \lambda v(p) \rangle \leq 0, \ \forall \lambda > 0. \tag{9}$$

I will now show that this implies that a competitive equilibrium price cannot exist. By contradiction. Let p^* be an equilibrium price and $x^* \in X^H$ be the corresponding equilibrium allocation. Consider $v(p^*) \in G_h(\Omega_h)$ satisfying (9). If $\lim_{\lambda \to \infty} u_h(\Omega_h + \lambda v(p)) = \infty$ this leads directly to a contradiction, because $\langle p^*, \lambda v(p^*) \rangle \leq 0$, so that for all λ, $\lambda v(p^*)$ is affordable, and therefore there is no affordable allocation which maximizes $h's$ utility at the equilibrium price p^*. Consider next the case where $v(p^*) \in G_h(\Omega_h) - A_h(\Omega_h)$. By definition, $u_h(\Omega_h + \lambda v(p^*))$ never ceases to increase in λ, and $\lim_{\lambda \to \infty} u_h(\Omega_h + \lambda v(p^*)) < \infty$. If $u_h(x_h^*) > \lim_{\lambda \to \infty} u_h(\Omega_h + \lambda v(p^*))$ then there exists a vector, namely x_h^*, which has utility strictly larger than $v(p^*) \in \partial G_h(\Omega_h)$ so that, as shown in Proposition 2, the direction defined by the vector $x^* - \Omega_h$ must be contained in $A_h(\Omega_h)$. But this contradicts the assumption that x_h^* is an equilibrium allocation, because if $x^* - \Omega_h \in A_h(\Omega_h)$, $\lim_{\lambda \to \infty} u_h(\Omega_h + \lambda(x_h^* - \Omega_h)) = \infty$, while $\langle p^*, \lambda(x_h^* - \Omega_h) \rangle \leq 0$ so that x_h^* cannot be an equilibrium allocation. Therefore limited arbitrage is also necessary for the existence of a competitive equilibrium in this case.

It remains to consider the case where $\exists p \in S(E)$ such that $\forall h \in \{1, ..., H\}$, $\langle p, \Omega_h \rangle \neq 0$. But in this case by definition $\bigcap_{h=1}^H D_h^+(\Omega_h) \neq \emptyset$ since $\forall h \in \{1...H\}$, $R_{++}^N \subset D_h^+(\Omega_h)$, so that limited arbitrage is always satisfied when an equilibrium exists. This completes the proof of necessity.

Sufficiency next. The proof uses the fact that the Pareto frontier is homeomorphic to a simplex. When $X = R_+^N$ the Pareto frontier of the economy $P(E)$ is always homeomorphic to a simplex, see [2]. In the case $X = R^N$ this may fail. However, by Theorem 1 above, if the economy satisfies limited arbitrage then the Pareto frontier is compact; under the assumptions on preferences, it is then also homeomorphic to a simplex [2]. Therefore in both cases, $P(\mathsf{E})$ is homeomorphic to a simplex and one can apply the by now standard Negishi method of using a fixed point argument on the Pareto frontier to establish the existence of a **pseudoequilibrium**.[42] It remains however to prove that the pseudoequilibrium is also a competitive equilibrium.

To complete the proof of existence of a competitive equilibrium consider first $X = R^N$. Then $\forall h = 1, ..., H$ there exists an allocation in X of strictly lower value than the pseudoequilibrium x_h^* at the price p^*. Therefore by Lemma 3, Chapter 4, page 81 of [2], the quasi-equilibrium (p^*, x^*) is also a competitive equilibrium, completing the proof of existence when $X = R^N$.

Next consider $X = R_+^N$, and a quasi-equilibrium (p^*, x^*) whose existence was already established. If every individual has a positive income at p^*, i.e., $\forall h$, $\langle p^*, \Omega_h \rangle > 0$, then by Lemma 3, Chapter 4 of [2] the quasi-equilibrium (p^*, x^*) is also a competitive equilibrium, completing the proof. Furthermore, observe that in any case the pseudoequilibrium price $p^* \in S(\mathsf{E})$, so that $S(\mathsf{E})$ is not empty. To prove existence we consider therefore two cases: first the case where $\exists q^* \in S(\mathsf{E}) : \forall h$, $\langle q^*, \Omega_h \rangle > 0$. In this case, by the above remarks from [2], (q^*, x^*) is a competitive equilibrium. The second case is when $\forall q \in S(\mathsf{E}), \exists h \in \{1, ..., H\}$ such that $\langle q, \Omega_h \rangle = 0$. Limited arbitrage then implies:

$$\exists q^* \in S(\mathsf{E}) : \ \forall h, \ \langle q^*, v \rangle > 0 \text{ for all } v \in G_h(\Omega_h). \tag{10}$$

Let $x^* = x_1^*, ..., x_H^* \in X^H$ be a feasible allocation in Υ supported by the vector q^* defined in (10): by definition, $\forall h$, $u_h(x_h^*) \geq u_h(\Omega_h)$ and q^* supports x^*. Note that any h minimizes costs at x_h^* because q^* is a support. Furthermore x_h^* is affordable under q^*. Therefore, (q^*, x^*) can fail to be a competitive equilibrium only when for some h, $\langle q^*, x_h^* \rangle = 0$, for otherwise the cost minimizing allocation is always also utility maximizing in the budget set $B_h(q^*) = \{w \in X : \langle q^*, w \rangle = \langle q^*, \Omega_h \rangle\}$.

It remains therefore to prove existence when $\langle q^*, x_h^* \rangle = 0$ for some h. Since by the definition of $S(\mathsf{E})$, x^* is individually rational, i.e., $\forall h$, $u_h(x_h^*) \geq u_h(\Omega_h)$, then $\langle q^*, x_h^* \rangle = 0$ implies $\langle q^*, \Omega_h \rangle = 0$, because by definition q^* is a supporting price for the equilibrium allocation x^*. If $\forall h$, $u_h(x_h^*) = 0$ then $x_h^* \in \partial R_+^N$, and by the monotonicity and quasi-concavity of u_h, any vector y in the budget set defined by the price p^*, $B_h(q^*)$, must also satisfy $u_h(y) = 0$, so that x_h^* maximizes utility in $B_h(q^*)$, which implies that (q^*, x^*) is a competitive equilibrium. Therefore (q^*, x^*) is a competitive equilibrium unless for some h, $u_h(x_h^*) > 0$.

Assume therefore that the quasiequilibrium (q^*, x^*) is not a competitive equilibrium, and that for some h with $\langle q^*, \Omega_h \rangle = 0, u_h(x_h^*) > 0$. Since $u_h(x_h^*) > 0$ and $x_h^* \in \partial R_+^N$ then an indifference surface of a commodity bundle of positive utility $u_h(x_h^*)$ intersects ∂R_+^N at $x_h^* \in \partial R_+^N$. Let r be the ray in ∂R_+^N containing x_h^*. If $w \in r$ then $\langle q^*, w \rangle = 0$, because $\langle q^*, x_h^* \rangle = 0$. Since $u_h(x_h^*) > 0$, by Proposition 3 u_h strictly increases along r, so that $w \in G_h(x_h^*)$. But this contradicts the choice of q^* as a supporting price satisfying limited arbitrage (10) since

$$\exists h \text{ and } w \in G_h(\Omega_h) \text{ such that } \langle q^*, w \rangle = 0. \tag{11}$$

The contradiction between (11) and (10) arose from the assumption that (q^*, x^*) is not a competitive equilibrium, so that (q^*, x^*) must be a competitive equilibrium, and the proof is complete.   □

5 Economies with infinitely many markets

The results of Theorem 2 are also valid for infinitely many markets. As already seen, the existence of inner products is useful in defining limited arbitrage. For this reason and because of the natural structure of prices in Hilbert spaces, I work on a Hilbert space of commodities in which inner products are defined.

5.1 Hilbert Spaces and the Cone Condition. All Hilbert spaces have positive orthants with empty interior. This can make things difficult when seeking to prove the existence of an equilibrium, which depends on finding supporting prices for efficient allocations. Supporting prices are usually found by applying the Hahn-Banach theorem, and without such prices a competitive equilibrium does not exist. Therefore the Hahn Banach theorem is crucial for proving existence of an equilibrium. However this theorem requires that the convex set being supported has a non-empty interior, a condition which is never satisfied within the positive orthant of a Hilbert space. This problem, which is typical in infinite dimensional spaces, was solved in 1980 by [26] who introduced a condition on preferences, the **cone condition (C-K,)**[43] and proved that it is necessary and sufficient for separating convex sets with or without non-empty interior, thus extending Hahn-Banach's theorem to encompass all convex sets, whether or not they have an empty interior. Since its introduction the **C-K cone condition** has been used extensively to prove the existence of a market equilibrium and in game theory; it is now a standard condition of economies with infinitely many markets and is known also under the name of "properness", cf., [15].

In addition to the cone condition, one more result is needed to extend directly the proof of Theorem 2 to economies with infinitely many markets: the compactness of the Pareto frontier. Recall that this frontier is always a finite dimensional object when there are a finite number of traders: it is contained in R_+^H, where H is the number of traders.

5.2 Limited Arbitrage and the Cone Condition. A somewhat unexpected result is that limited arbitrage implies the **C-K cone condition**, see [28, 30]. Because of this, limited arbitrage is necessary and sufficient for the existence of a competitive equilibrium and the core, with or without short sales, in the infinite dimensional space H. Limited arbitrage therefore unifies the treatment of finitely and infinitely many markets.

Consider an economy E as defined in Section 2 except that here $X = $ H or $X = $ H$^+$; more general convex sets can be considered as well, see [28, 30]. The global cones and the market cones, and the limited arbitrage condition, are the same as defined in the finite dimensional cases when $X = R^N$ and $X = R_+^N$ respectively. To shorten the presentation, here the market cones are assumed to be uniform across initial endowments, a condition which is automatically satisfied under Assumption 1 when $X = $ H, and which is not needed for the main results, cf., [28, 30]. Therefore here either limited is satisfied at every endowment or not at all. The results on existence of an equilibrium presented below are in [28, 30].

Definition 9 *The cone defined by a convex set $D \subset X$ at a point $x \in D$ is* $C(D,x) = \{z \in X : z = x + \lambda(y - x), \text{ where } \lambda > 0 \text{ and } y \in D\}.$

Definition 10 *A convex set $D \subset X$ satisfies the* **C-K cone condition** *of* [26] *at $x \in D$ when there exists a vector $v \in X$ which is at positive distance $\varepsilon(D,x)$ from the cone with vertex x defined by the set $D, C(D,x)$.*

Definition 11 *A preference* $u_h : X \to R$ *satisfies the* **C-K cone condition** *of* [**26**][44] *when for every* $x \in X$, *the preferred set* $u_h^x = \{y : u_h(y) \geq u_h(x)\} \subset X$ *of* u_h *at* x *satisfies the* C-K *condition, and* $\varepsilon(P_x, x)$ *is independent of* x.

The finite dimensional proofs work for infinite dimensions when X is a Hilbert space H, see [**28, 30**]. The only case which requires special treatment is $X = H^+$ because with infinite dimensional Hilbert spaces the positive orthant H^+ has empty interior:

Theorem 3 *(Chichilnisky and Heal) Consider an economy* E *as defined in Section 2, where the trading space is either* $X = H^+$, *or* $X = H$, *and where* H *is a Hilbert space of finite or infinite dimensions. Then limited arbitrage implies the* **C-K** [**26**] *cone condition. In particular, the second welfare theorem applies under limited arbitrage: a Pareto efficient allocation is also a competitive equilibrium.*

Proof For a proof see [**28, 30**]. An outline of the proof for $X = H^+$ follows. The case $X = H$ is in [**28**] and [**30**] and follows directly from the finite dimensional case.

Let $X = H^+$: I will show first that limited arbitrage, as defined in Section 2, implies that there exists a vector $p \neq 0$ in $S(\mathsf{E})$. The proof is by contradiction. If $\sim \exists p \neq 0$ in $S(\mathsf{E})$, then the intersection of the dual cones in Definition 6 must be empty, i.e., $\cap_{h=1}^{H} D_h^+ = \emptyset$: this occurs either because for some h, the set $D_h^+ = D_h \cap S(\mathsf{E})$ is empty, or alternatively because the set $S(\mathsf{E})$ itself is empty. In either case this leads to a contradiction with limited arbitrage which requires that $\cap_{h=1}^{H} D_h^+ \neq \emptyset$. Since the contradiction arises from assuming that $\sim \exists p \neq 0$ in $S(\mathsf{E})$, it follows that $\exists p \in S(\mathsf{E}), p \neq 0$, i.e., the preferred set of u_h can be supported by a non-zero price p at some x_h which is part of a feasible affordable efficient and individually rational allocation, $x = x_1, ..., x_H$.

The last step is to show that there exists one vector v, the same for all traders, which is at a positive distance ε from $C(u_h^x, x)$ *for every trader* h as well as for every $x \in X$. Consider now the vector $v = \sum_{h=1}^{H} p_h$, where p_h is the support whose existence was established above, and let $\varepsilon = \min_{i=1,2,...,H}\{\varepsilon_i\}$. The vector v satisfies the definition of the cone condition C-K.[45] $\qquad\square$

Theorem 4 *(Chichilnisky and Heal) Consider an economy* E *as defined in Section 2, where* $X = H$, *or* $X = H^+$, *where* H *is a Hilbert space of finite or infinite dimensions. Then limited arbitrage is necessary and sufficient for the compactness of the Pareto frontier.*

Proof Since the cone condition holds, the proof is a straightforward extension of Theorem 1 which holds for the finite dimensional case. See [**28, 30**]. $\qquad\square$

Theorem 5 *(Chichilnisky and Heal) Consider an economy* E *as defined in Section 2, where* $X = H^+$ *or* $X = H$, *a Hilbert space of finite or infinite dimensions. Then limited arbitrage is necessary and sufficient for the existence of a competitive equilibrium.*

Proof The proof is similar to that for the finite dimensional case, see [**28, 30**]. $\qquad\square$

5.3 Subeconomies with Competitive Equilibria. The condition of limited arbitrage need not be tested on all traders simultaneously: in the case of R^N, it needs only be satisfied on subeconomies with no more traders than the number of commodities in the economy,[46] N, plus one.

Definition 12 *A $k-$trader sub-economy of* E *is an economy* F *consisting of a subset of $k \leq H$ traders in* E, *each with the endowments and preferences as in* E: $F = \{X, u_h, \Omega_h, h \in J \subset \{1, ..., H\}, \text{ cardinality } (J) = k \leq H\}.$

Theorem 6 *The following four properties of an economy* E *with trading space R^N are equivalent:*

(i) E *has a competitive equilibrium*

(ii) Every sub economy of E *with at most $N + 1$ traders has a competitive equilibrium*

(iii) E *has limited arbitrage*

(iv) E *has limited arbitrage for any subset of traders with no more that $N + 1$ members.*

Proof Theorem 1 implies (i)⇔(iii) and (ii)⇔(iv). That (iii)⇔(iv) follows from the following theorem which is a corollary in [**17**]: Consider a family $\{U_i\}_{i=1...H}$ of convex sets in R^N, $H, N \geq 1$. Then

$$\bigcap_{i=1}^{H} U_i \neq \emptyset \text{ if and only if } \bigcap_{j \in J} U_i \neq \emptyset$$

for any subset of indices $J \subset \{1...H\}$ having at most $N + 1$ elements.

In particular, an economy E as defined in Section 2 satisfies limited arbitrage, if and only if it satisfies limited arbitrage for any subset of $k = N + 1$ traders, where N is the number of commodities in the economy E. □

6 Limited arbitrage equilibrium and the core with finitely or infinitely many markets

Limited arbitrage is also necessary and sufficient for the nonemptiness of the core:[44]

Theorem 7 *Consider an economy* E $= \{X, u_h, \Omega_h, h = 1, ..., H\}$, *where $H \geq 2$, $X = R^N$ and $N \geq 1$, or X is a Hilbert space H. Then the following three properties are equivalent:*

(i) The economy E *has limited arbitrage*

(ii) The economy E *has a core*

(iii) Every subeconomy of E with at most $N + 1$ trades has a core

Proof For the proof of (i)⇔(ii) and a discussion of the literature see [**19**]. The equivalence (i)⇔(iii) then follows from Theorem 6. □

7 Social diversity and the supercore

The supercore was defined and motivated in Section 1.2. It measures the extent to which a society has reasons to stay together. Social diversity comes in many shades, one of which, the mildest possible, will be used to establish the existence of a supercore:

Definition 13 *An economy* E *is socially diverse when it does not satisfy limited arbitrage. When $X = R^N$, this means:*

$$\bigcap_{h=1}^{H} D_h = \emptyset.$$

When $X = R_+^N$:

$$\bigcap_{h=1}^{H} D_h^+(\Omega_h) = \emptyset.$$

In this section short sales are allowed, so that the trading space is $X = R^N$. To simplify notation assume without loss of generality that all endowments are zero, $\forall h$, $\Omega_h = 0$. Assume now that the normalized gradients of closed sets of indifferent vectors define closed sets (case (ii)) so that[48] $G_h = A_h$.

Definition 14 E *has social diversity of type 1, or* SD1, *when all subeconomies with at most $H - 1$ traders have limited arbitrage, but* E *does not.*

Theorem 8 *Consider an economy* E *with at least three traders. Then if* E *has social diversity of type 1,* SD1, *its supercore is not empty.*

Proof Since the economy has social diversity of type 1, every subeconomy of $H - 1$ traders satisfies limited arbitrage, which by Proposition 4 implies that gains from trade G(E) are bounded in every $H - 1$ trader subeconomy. In particular, there is a maximum level of utility which each trader can obtain by him or herself, and the same is true for any subgroup consisting of at most $H - 1$ traders.

However, by Proposition 4, gains from trade cannot be bounded in E for the set of all H traders, since E does not satisfy limited arbitrage.   □

8 Limited arbitrage and social choice

Limited arbitrage is also crucial for resource allocation via social choice. Two main approaches to social choice are studied here. One is Arrow's: his axioms of social choice require that the social choice rule Φ be non-dictatorial, independent of irrelevant alternatives, and satisfy a Pareto condition [1]. A second approach introduced in [7] and [9] requires, instead, that the rule Φ be continuous, anonymous, and respect unanimity. Both approaches have led to corresponding impossibility results [1, 7, 9]. Though the two sets of axioms are quite different, it has been shown recently that the impossibility results which emerge from them are equivalent, see [4]. Furthermore, as is shown below, limited arbitrage is closely connected with both sets of axioms. Economies which satisfy limited arbitrage admit social choice rules with either set of axioms. In a well defined sense, the social choice problem can only be solved in those economies which satisfy limited arbitrage.

How do we allocate resources by social choice? Social choice rules assign a social preference $\Phi(u_1...u_H)$ to each list $(u_1...u_H)$ of individual preferences of an economy E.[45] The social preference ranks allocations in $R^{N \times H}$, and allows to select an optimal feasible allocation. This is the resource allocation obtained via social choice.

The procedure requires, of course, that a social choice rule Φ exists: the role of limited arbitrage is important because it ensures existence. This will be established below. I prove here that limited arbitrage is necessary and sufficient for resolving Arrow's paradox when the domain of individual preferences are those in the economy, and the choices are those feasible allocations which give large utility value.[47]

Limited arbitrage provides a restriction on the relationship between individual preferences under which social choice rules exist. A brief background on the matter of preference diversity follows.

Arrow's impossibility theorem established that in general a social choice rule Φ does not exist: the problem of social choice has no solution unless individual preferences are restricted. Duncan Black in [5] established that the "single peakedness" of preferences is a sufficient restriction to obtain majority rules. Using different axioms, [7, 9] established also that a social choice rule Φ does not generally exist; subsequently Chichilnisky and Heal in [27] established a necessary and sufficient restriction for the resolution of the social choice paradox: the *contractibility* of the space of preferences.[47] Contractibility can be interpreted as a limitation on preference diversity, [36]. In all cases, therefore, the problem of social choice is resolved by restricting the diversity of individual preferences. The main result in this section is that the restriction on individual preferences required to solve the problem is precisely limited arbitrage. The connection between limited arbitrage and contractibility is discussed below.

The section is organized as follows. First I show in Proposition 6 that the economy E satisfies limited arbitrage if and only if it contains no *Condorcet cycles* on choices of large utility values.[48] Condorcet cycles are the building blocks of Arrow's impossibility theorem, and are at the root of the social choice problem. On the basis of Proposition 6, I prove in Theorem 9 that limited arbitrage is necessary and sufficient for resolving Arrow's paradox on allocations of large utility values.

Definition 15 *A Condorcet cycle is a collection of three preferences over a choice set X, represented by three utilities $u_i : X \to R$, $i = 1, 2, 3$, and three choices α, β, γ within a feasible set $Y \subset X$ such that $u_1(\alpha) > u_1(\beta) > u_1(\gamma)$, $u_2(\gamma) > u_2(\alpha) > u_2(\beta)$ and $u_3(\beta) > u_3(\gamma) > u_3(\alpha)$.*

Within an economy with finite resources $\Omega >> 0$, the social choice problem is about the choice of allocations of these resources. Choices are in $X = R^{N \times H}$. An allocation $(x_1...x_H) \in R^{N \times H}$ is *feasible* if $\sum_i x_i - \Omega = 0$. Consider an economy E as defined in Section 2. Preferences over private consumption are increasing, $u_h(x) > u_h(y)$ if $x > y \in R^N$, utilities are uniformly non-satiated (Assumption 1), and indifference surfaces which are not bounded below have a closed set of gradients,[49] so that $G_h = A_h$. While the preferences in E are defined over private consumption, they naturally define preference over allocations, as follows: define $u_h(x_1...x_H) \geq u_h(y_i...y_H) \Leftrightarrow u_h(x_h) \geq u_h(y_h)$. Thus the preferences in the economy E induce naturally preferences over the feasible allocations in E.

Definition 16 *The family of preferences $\{u_1...u_H\}$, $u_h : R^N \to R$ of an economy E has a Condorcet cycle of size k if for every three preferences $u_1^k, u_2^k, u_3^k \in \{u_1...u_H\}$ there exist three feasible allocations $\alpha^k = (\alpha_1^k, \alpha_2^k, \alpha_3^k) \in X^3 \subset R^{3 \times N}$; $\beta^k = (\beta_1^k, \beta_2^k, \beta_3^k)$ and $\gamma^k = (\gamma_1^k, \gamma_2^k, \gamma_3^k)$ which define a Condorcet cycle, and such that each trader $h = 1, ..., H$, achieves at least a utility level k at each choice:*

$$\min_{h=1,...,H} \{[u_h^k(\alpha_h^k), u_h^k(\beta_h^k), u_h^k(\gamma_h^k)]\} > k.$$

The following shows that limited arbitrage eliminates Condorcet cycles on matters of great importance, namely on those with utility level approaching the supremum of the utilities, which by appropriate choice of utility representations and without loss of generality we have assumed to be ∞ :

Proposition 6 *Let E be a market economy with short sales $(X = R^N)$ and $H \geq 3$ traders. Then E has social diversity if and only if its traders' preferences have Condorcet cycles of every size. Equivalently, E has limited arbitrage if and* *only for some $k > 0$, the traders' preferences have no Condorcet cycles of size larger than k.*

Proof Consider an economy with Condorcet cycles of all sizes. For each $k > 0$, there exist three allocations denoted $(\alpha^k, \beta^k, \gamma^k) \in R^{3 \times N \times H}$ and three traders $u_{k_1}^k, u_{k_2}^k, u_{k_3}^k \subset \{u_1 ... u_H\}$ which define a Condorcet triple of size k. By definition, for every k, each of the three allocations is feasible, for example, $\alpha^k = (\alpha_1^k, ..., \alpha_H^k) \in R^{N \times H}$, and $\sum_{i=1}^{H}(\alpha_i^k) = 0$. Furthermore, $\min_{h=1,...,H}\{[u_h^k(\alpha_h^k), u_h^k(\beta_h^k), u_h(\gamma_h^k)]\} > k$, so that $\forall h \lim_{k \to \infty} (u_h(\alpha_h^k)) = \infty$. In particular, there exist a sequence of allocations $(\theta^k)_{k=1,2...} = (\theta_1^k, ..., \theta_H^k)_{k=1,2...}$ such that $\forall k$, $\sum_{h=1}^{H} \theta_h^k = 0$ and $\forall h \sup_{k \to \infty} u_h(\theta_h^k) = \infty$. This implies that E has unbounded gains from trade, which contradicts Proposition 3. Therefore E cannot have Condorcet cycles of every size.

Conversely, if E has no limited arbitrage, for any $k > 0$, there exist a feasible allocation $(a_1^k, a_2^k, ..., a_H^k)$, such that $\sum_{h=1}^{H} a_h^k \leq 0$, and $\forall h$, $u_h(a_h^k) \geq k$. For each integer $k > 0$, and for a small enough $\varepsilon > 0$ define now the vector $\Delta = (\varepsilon, ..., \varepsilon) \in R_+^N$ and the following three allocations: $\alpha^k = (ka_1^k, ka_2^k - 2\Delta, ka_3^k + 2\Delta, ka_4^k, ..., ka_H^k)$, $\beta^k = (ka_1^k - \Delta, ka_2^k, ka_3^k + \Delta, ka_4^k, ..., ka_H^k)$ and $\gamma^k = (ka_1^k - 2\Delta, ka_2^k - \Delta, ka_3^k + 3\Delta, ka_4^k, ..ka_H^k)$. Each allocation is feasible, e.g., $ka_1^k + ka_2^k - 2\Delta + ka_3^k + 2\Delta + ka_4^k + ... + ka_H^k = k(\sum_{h=1}^{H} a_h^k) \leq 0$. Furthermore, for each $k > 0$ sufficiently large, the three allocations $\alpha^k, \beta^k, \gamma^k$ and the traders $h = 1, 2, 3$, define a Condorcet cycle of size k: all traders except for $1, 2, 3$, are indifferent between the three allocations and they reach a utility value at least k, while trader 1 prefers α^k to β^k to γ^k, trader 3 prefers γ^k to α^k to β^k, and trader 2 prefers β^k to γ^k to α^k. Observe that this construction can be made for any three traders within the set $\{1, 2, ..., H\}$. This completes the proof. ☐

The next result uses Proposition 6 to establish the connection between limited arbitrage and Arrow's theorem. Consider Arrow's three axioms: Pareto, independence of irrelevant alternatives, and non-dictatorship. The social choice problem is to find a social choice rule $\Phi : P^j \to P$ from individual to social preferences satisfying Arrow's three axioms; the domain for the rule Φ are profiles of individual preferences over allocations of the economy E: $\Phi : P^j \to P$. Recall that each preference in the economy E defines a preference over feasible allocations in E.

Definition 17 *The economy E admits a resolution of Arrow's paradox if for any number of voters $j \geq 3$ there exists a social choice function from the space $P = \{u_1, ..., u_H\}$ of preferences of the economy E into the space Q of complete transitive preference defined on the space of feasible allocations of E, $\Phi : P^j \to Q$, satisfying Arrow's three axioms.*

Definition 18 *A feasible allocation $(\alpha_1^k, ..., \alpha_H^k) \in R^{N \times H}$ has utility value k, or simply value k, if each trader achieves at least a utility level k :*

$$\min_{h \in H}\{[u_1^k(\alpha_1^k), ..., u_H(\alpha_H^k)]\} > k.$$

Definition 19 *Arrow's paradox is said to be resolved on choices of large utility value in the economy E when for all $j \geq 3$ there exists social choice function $\Phi : P^j \to Q$ and a $k > 0$ such that Φ is defined on all profiles of j preferences in E, and it satisfies Arrow's three axioms when restricted to allocations of utility value exceeding k.[50]*

Theorem 9 *Limited arbitrage is necessary and sufficient for a resolution of Arrow's paradox on choices of large utility value in the economy E.*

Proof Necessity follows from Proposition 6, since by Arrow's axiom of independence of irrelevant alternatives, the existence of one Condorcet triple of size k suffices to produce Arrow's impossibility theorem on feasible choices of value k in our domain of preferences, see [1]. Sufficiency is immediate: limited arbitrage eliminates feasible allocation of large utility value by Proposition 1, because it bounds gains from trade. Therefore it resolves Arrow's paradox, because this is automatically resolved in an empty domain of choices. □

8.1 Social choice rules which are continuous, anonymous and respect unanimity. Consider now the second approach to social choice, introduced in [7, 9], which seeks continuous anonymous social choice rules which respect unanimity. The link connecting arbitrage with social choices is still very close but it takes a different form. In this case the connection is between the contractibility of the space of preferences, which is necessary and sufficient for the existence of continuous, anonymous rules which respect unanimity [27] and limited arbitrage.

Continuity is defined in a standard manner; anonymity means that the social preference does not depend on the order of voting. Respect of unanimity means that if all individuals have identical preferences overall, so does the social preference; it is a very weak version of the Pareto condition. It was shown in [7, 9] that, for general spaces of preferences, there exist no social choice rules satisfying these three axioms. Subsequently, Chichilnisky and Heal in [27] established that contractibility is exactly what is needed for the existence of social choice rules. It is worth observing that *the following result is valid for any topology on the space of preferences T*. In this sense this result is analogous to a fixed point theorem or to a maximization theorem: whatever the topology, a continuous function from a compact convex space to itself has a fixed point and a continuous function of a compact set has a maximum. All these statements, and the one below, apply independently of the topology chosen:

Theorem 10 *Let T be a connected space of preferences endowed with any topology.[51] Then T admits a continuous anonymous map Φ respecting unanimity*

$$\Phi : T^k \to T$$

for every $k \geq 2$, if and only if T is contractible.

Proof See [27]. □

The close relation between contractibility and non-empty intersection (which is limited arbitrage) follows from the following theorem:

Theorem 11 *Let $\{U_i\}_{i=1...I}$ be a family of convex sets in R^N. The family has a non-empty intersection if and only if every subfamily has a contractible union:*

$$\bigcap_{i=1}^{I} U_i \neq \phi \Leftrightarrow \bigcup_{i \in J} U_i \text{ is contractible } \forall J \subset \{1...I\}.$$

Proof See [7] and [15]. □

This theorem holds for general excisive families of sets, including acyclic families and even *simple families* which consist of sets which need not be convex, acyclic, open or even connected. This theorem was shown to imply the Knaster Kuratowski Marzukiewicz theorem and Brouwer's fixed point theorem [15], but it is not implied by them. Theorem 11 establishes a close link between contractibility and non-empty intersection and is used to show that limited arbitrage, or equivalently the lack of social diversity, is necessary and sufficient for resource allocation via social choice rules.

Intuitively, a preference is similar to that of trader h when it ranks higher those allocations which assign h a consumption vector which u_h prefers. In mathematical terms this means that the space of preferences similar to those of a subset J of traders in the economy have gradients within the union of the market cones of the traders in J. Formally, let the space of choices be R^N and define a space of preferences as follows:

Definition 20 *Let P_J consist of all those preferences which are similar to those of the market economy* E, *in the sense that their gradients are in the union of the market cones of the traders in J, see* [11, 12]

$$P_J = \{u : u \text{ defines a preference on } R^N \text{ satisfying Assumption 1, and}$$

$$\exists J \subset \{1, ..., H\} : \forall x \in R^N, Du(x) \in \cup_{h \in J} D_h\}.$$

In the following we assume that the set P_J is connected, for which it suffices that any two traders would wish to trade.[52]

Theorem 12 *The economy E satisfies limited arbitrage if and only if for any subset of traders $J \subset \{1, 2, ..., H\}$ the union of all market cones $\cup_{h \in J} D_h$ is contractible.*

Proof This follows directly from Theorem 11.   □

Theorem 13 *There exists a continuous anonymous social choice rule Φ : $P_J^k \rightarrow P_J$ which respects unanimity for every $k \geq 2$ and every $J \subset \{1, ..., H\}$ if and only if the economy E has limited arbitrage, i.e. if and only if the economy has a competitive equilibrium and a non-empty core.*

Proof See [11, 12], Theorems 2, 7, 10 and 12.   □

9 Social diversity and limited arbitrage

If the economy does not have limited arbitrage, it is called **socially diverse**:

Definition 21 *The economy* E *is* **socially diverse** *when $\bigcap_{h=1}^{H} D_h = \phi$.*

This concept is robust under small errors in measurement and is independent of the units of measurement or choice of numeraire. If E is not socially diverse, all economies sufficiently close in endowments and preferences have the same property: the concept is **structurally stable**. Social diversity admits different "shades"; these can be measured, for example, by the smallest number of market cones which do not intersect:

Definition 22 *The economy* E *has* **index of diversity** *$I(E) = H - K$ if $K+1$ is the smallest number such that $\exists J \subset \{1...H\}$ with cardinality of $J = K + 1$, and $\bigcap_{h \in J} D_h = \phi$. The index $I(E)$ ranges between 0 and $H - 1$: the larger the index, the larger the social diversity. The index is smallest when all the market cones intersect: then all social diversity disappears, and the economy has limited arbitrage.*

Theorem 14 *The index of social diversity is $I(E)$ if and only if $H - I(E)$ is the maximum number of traders for which every subeconomy with such a number of traders has a competitive equilibrium, a non-empty core, admits social choice rules which satisfy Arrow's axioms on choices giving large utility values, and admits social* *choice rules which are continuous, anonymous and respect unanimity on preferences similar to those of the subeconomy.*

10 A topological invariant for the market E

This section shows that the resource allocation properties of the economy E can be described simply in terms of the properties of a family of cohomology rings denoted $CH(\mathsf{E})$.

A ring is a set Q endowed with two operations, denoted $+$ and $\times$; the operation $+$ must define a group structure for Q (every element has an inverse under $+$) and the operation $\times$ defined a semigroup structure for Q; both operations together satisfy an associative relation. A typical example of a ring is the set of the integers, as well as the rational numbers, both with addition and multiplication.

The *cohomology ring* of a space Y contains information about the space's topological structure, namely those properties of the space which remain invariant when the space is deformed as if it was made of rubber. For a formal definition see [**45**]. An intuitive explanation is as follows. The cohomology ring consists of maps defined on homology groups. Intuitively a homology group consists of "holes", defined as cycles which do not bound any region in the space Y. The homology groups are indexed by dimension. For example the circle S^1 has the simplest possible "hole": its first homology group measures that. The "torus" $S_1 \times S_1$ has two types of holes: therefore it has a non-zero first homology group as well as a non-zero second homology group. Any convex, or contractible, space has no "holes" so that its cohomology groups are all zero. In addition to the standard group structure of each cohomology group, there is another operation, called a "cup product", which consists, intuitively, of "patching up" elements across cohomology groups. The set of all cohomology groups with these two operations defines the cohomology ring.

The rings $CH(\mathsf{E})$ are the cohomology rings corresponding to subfamilies of market cones $\{D_h\}$ of the economy E define a topological invariant of the economy E in the sense that they are the same for any continuous deformation of the space of commodities on which the economy is defined, i.e., they are preserved under any continuous transformation in the units of measurement of the commodities. They are also preserved under small perturbations of, or measurement errors on, the traders' preferences.

Definition 23 *The* **nerve** *of a family of subsets* $\{V_i\}_{i=1,\ldots,L}$, *in* R^M,[53] *denoted*

$$nerve\{V_i\}_{i=1,\ldots,L}$$

is a simplicial complex defined as follows: each subfamily of $k+1$ sets in $\{V_i\}_{i=1,\ldots,L}$ with non-empty intersection is a $k-simplex$ of the nerve$\{V_i\}_{i=1,\ldots,L}$.

A **subfamily** of the family of sets $\{D_h\}_{h=1,\ldots,H}$ is a family consisting of some of the sets in $\{D_h\}_{h=1,\ldots,H}$ and is indicated $\{D_h\}_{h\in Q}$ where $Q \subset \{1,\ldots,H\}$.

The **topological invariant** $CH(\mathsf{E})$ of the economy E with $X = R^N$ is the family of reduced cohomology rings[54] of the simplicial complexes defined by all subfamilies $\{D_h\}_{h\in Q}$ of the family $\{D_h\}_{h=1,2\ldots H}$, i.e., the cohomology rings of $\{nerve\{D_h\}_{h\in G}$ for every $Q \subset \{1,\ldots,H\}$.

$$CH(\mathsf{E})\{H^*(nerve\{D_h\}_{h\in Q}, \forall Q \subset \{1,\ldots,H\}\}.$$

For the following result I consider continuous deformations of the economy which preserve its convexity and Assumption 1.

Theorem 15 *The economy* E *with* H *traders has limited arbitrage, and therefore a competitive equilibrium, a non-empty core and social choice rules if and only if:*

$$CH(\mathsf{E}) = 0$$

i.e., $\forall Q \subset \{1, \dots, \mathsf{H}\}, \mathsf{H}^*(nerve\{D_h\}_{h \in q}) = 0.$

Furthermore, the economy E has social diversity index $I(\mathsf{E})$ if and only if $I(E) = H - K$, where K satisfies the following conditions: (i) for every $\{F_h\} \in \{D_h\}$ of cardinality at most K

$$\mathsf{H}^*(nerve\{D_h\}_{h \in Q}) = 0,$$

and there exists $T \subset \{1, \dots, \mathsf{H}\}$ with cardinality $T = K + 1$ and

$$\mathsf{H}^*(nerve\{D_h\}_{h \in T}) \neq 0.$$

Proof This follows directly from [**17**].   □

11 Related literature on market equilibrium

The literature on the existence of a competitive (Walrasian) market equilibrium is about fifty years old, starting with the classic works of Von-Neumann, Nash, Arrow and Debreu and others. This literature has focussed on sufficient conditions for existence rather than on necessary and sufficient conditions as studied here. It can be reviewed in two parts: markets without short sales, such as those studied by Arrow and Debreu, and markets with short sales which appear in the literature on financial markets.

11.1 Related Literature on Equilibrium with Bounds on Short Sales.
Two well known conditions are sufficient for the existence of an equilibrium[55] when $X = R_+^N$. They are Arrow's "resource relatedness" condition [**2**], and McKenzie's "irreducibility" condition [**40, 41, 42**]; both are sufficient but neither is necessary for existence. Both imply limited arbitrage, which is simultaneously necessary and sufficient for the existence of a competitive equilibrium. Resource relatedness and irreducibility ensure existence by requiring that the endowments of any trader are desired, directly or indirectly, by others, so that the traders' incomes cannot fall to zero. Under these conditions it is easy to check that limited arbitrage is always satisfied, and a competitive equilibrium always exists. Yet traders with zero or minimum income do not by themselves rule out the existence of a competitive equilibrium. Limited arbitrage could be satisfied even when some traders have zero income. This reflects a real situation: some individuals are considered economically worthless, in that they have nothing to offer that others want in a market context. Such a situation could be a competitive equilibrium. Figure 8 provides an example. It seems realistic that markets could lead to such allocations: one observes them all the time in city ghettos. Limited arbitrage does not attempt to rule out individuals with minimum (or zero) income; instead, it seeks to determine if society's evaluation of their worthlessness is shared. Individuals are diverse in the sense of not satisfying limited arbitrage, when someone has minimal (or zero) income, and, in addition, when there is no agreement about the value of those who have minimal income. In such cases there is no competitive equilibrium.

Another condition which is sufficient but not necessary for existence of a competitive equilibrium is that the indifference surfaces of preferences of positive consumption bundles should be in the interior of the positive orthant, [**31**]: this implies that the set of directions along which the utilities increase without bound from initial endowments is the same for all traders. Therefore all individuals agree on choices with large utility values, again a form of similarity of preferences. It is immediate to see that such economies satisfy limited arbitrage.

11.2 Related Literature on Equilibrium in Markets With Short Sales.

The literature of general equilibrium with short sales has concentrated on sufficient conditions for existence, for example [35], [37], [34], [27, 29], and not on the question of conditions which are simultaneously necessary and sufficient for existence as studied here and previously in [11, 13, 18, 22] and [28] and [29]. In addition, the literature has neglected economies where the feasible individually rational allocations do not form a compact set. Previous sufficient results for the existence of an equilibrium in economies with short sales rely on the fact that the set of feasible allocations is compact. Theorem 2 above (see also [11, 13, 18, 22]) and [28], and [29] is original in that it provides conditions which are necessary and sufficient for existence in economies where feasible and individually rational allocations may be unbounded; in addition these results are novel in that they apply in economies with or without short sales, and for finitely or infinitely many markets.

In the context of temporary equilibrium models, which are different from Arrow Debreu models because forward markets are missing, [33] established early on interesting, necessary and sufficient conditions on "overlapping expectations" for the existence of a temporary equilibrium; similar conditions appear in [32] also in the context of temporary equilibrium and Green's model. Sufficient conditions for existence in economies with short sales, i.e., when $X = R^N$, include those of [32], which requires the "irreversibility" of the total consumption set $X = \sum_{h=1}^{H} X_h$: this contrasts with limited arbitrage in that it applies to the whole consumption set X rather than to global or market cones, in any case it is only a sufficient condition for existence. Other "no arbitrage" conditions have been used, for example in the finance literature. The connection between the standard notion of no-arbitrage and limited arbitrage, was discussed in Section 2.2. The no-arbitrage Condition C of [27, 29] is an antecedent for limited arbitrage: it is a no-arbitrage condition which is sufficient but not necessary in general for the existence of a competitive equilibrium; it requires that along a sequence of feasible allocations where the utility of one trader increases beyond bound, there exists another trader whose utility eventually decreases below this trader's utility at the initial endowment. This result is based on a bounded set of feasible allocations, a conditions need not be satisfied in this paper.

Another condition of no-arbitrage based on recession cones appears in [46] and in [44], who provide sufficient conditions for the existence of an equilibrium in finite dimensions. The results of [46] and [44] are posterior and less general than those in those in[56] [27, 29]; they are restricted to finite dimensional economies with short sales and with strictly convex preferences, and are based on bounded sets of feasible allocations. The same no-arbitrage condition based on recession cones had been previously used for special models of asset prices with strictly convex preferences, which are incomplete markets and exclude also the Arrow Debreu treatment of short sales. The no-arbitrage condition mentioned above is sufficient but not necessary in general economies for the existence of an equilibrium. Under certain conditions which exclude the Arrow Debreu treatment of short sales, and which exclude also the case of preferences which are not strictly convex and which may have different recession cones at different endowments, conditions which are not required here, Werner [46] provides two conditions, one which is proved to be sufficient for existence of equilibrium and another which is mentioned without formal statement or proof to be necessary for existence. The two conditions involve different cones, and there is no complete proof in [46] that the two cones, and therefore the two conditions, are the same. However, the two cones in [46] coincide in very special cases: for example, when recession cones are uniform and equal to directions of strict utility increase and when indifferences contain no halflines, conditions which are not required here. In the general case there is no complete proof in [46] that his two cones, and therefore his two conditions, are the same; the details are in Section 4 above. No-arbitrage as defined in [46] is not defined on initial parameters of the economy: it must be verified in principle at all allocations, thus eliminating cases where limited arbitrage is satisfied (with the same preferences) for some initial endowments and not for others, cases which are included in the analysis of this paper.

12 Conclusions

One limitation on social diversity, limited arbitrage, is necessary and sufficient for the existence of a competitive equilibrium, the core and social choice rules in Arrow Debreu economies [3]. Social diversity is however more subtle and complex: it comes in many shades. Social diversity is zero when limited arbitrage is satisfied, and it is defined generally in terms of the properties of the cohomology rings CH of the nerve of a family of cones which are naturally associated with the economy. The cohomology rings of these nerves contain information about which subeconomies have competitive equilibria and a core, and which have social choice rules; the mildest form of social diversity is sufficient for the existence of a supercore, which consists of all those allocations which no strict subcoalition has a reason to block.

From these results an implicit prediction emerges about the characteristics of economies which have evolved mechanisms to allocate resources efficiently according to markets, cooperative game solutions, or social choice: they will exhibit only a limited amount of social diversity. Economies which do not succeed in allocating resource efficiently are not likely to be observed in practice, so that existing economies are likely to exhibit limited social diversity.

Other forms of diversity come to mind—for example, the genetic diversity of a population: this is generally believed to be favorable for the species' survival. In the biological context, therefore, diversity is a positive feature. This may appear to run counter to what is said here. Not so. Some diversity is desirable in economics as well: as mentioned at the beginning of this paper, without diversity there would be no gains from trade. Indeed without diversity the market would have no reason to exist. The matter is subtle: in the end, it is a question of degrees, of how much diversity is desirable or acceptable.

The tenet of this paper is that the economic organizations which prevail today require a well-defined amount of diversity, and no more, to function properly. One is led to consider the following, somewhat unsettling, question: is it possible that existing forms of economic organization restrict diversity beyond what would be desirable for the survival of our species? Or, more generally: are the forms of social and economic organization which prevail in our society sustainable?

13 Notes

1. The core is an allocation which no subset of players can improve upon within their own endowments.

2. Limited arbitrage was introduced and named in [**11, 13, 17, 18, 19, 20, 22, 23**] and [**28**].

3. No-arbitrage is discussed in Section 2.2.

4. These results were first established in [**11, 13, 17, 19, 20, 22, 23, 19**].

5. This result was first established in [**28**].

6. This result and its proof were presented at the Econometric Society Meetings in Boston, January 3-5, 1994.

7. A result first established in [**11, 12, 17**].

8. CH is defined in Section 10.

9. It is possible to use lesser concepts of equilibrium, such as quasiequilibrium and compensated equilibrium, or equilibria where there may be excess supply in the economy. These exist under quite general conditions, but fail to provide Pareto efficient allocations and are therefore less attractive from the point of view of resource allocation, so they are not used here. The relationship between limited arbitrage and quasiequilibrium is explored further in [**24**].

10. I.e. whether trades are bounded below or not.

11. Contractibility ensures that the preferences of all traders can be continuously deformed into one and is therefore a form of similarity of preferences, see [**36**].

12. This theorem is also valid for non-convex excisive families of sets [**7, 17**], and is shown in to imply Brower's fixed point theorem, the KKM theorem, Caratheodory's theorem and Leray's theorem, but it is not implied by them.

13. In [**8, 15**], a result which has Helly's theorem as a corollary.

14. Arrow and Debreu's formalization of markets assume that the consumption sets of the individuals are bounded below, an assumption motivated by the inability of humans to provide more than a fixed number of hours of labor per day.

15. Chichilnisky and Heal in [**28, 29, 30**] proved that limited arbitrage is necessary and sufficient for the existence of a competitive equilibrium in economies with infinitely many markets.

16. I work within a standard framework where preferences are convex and uniformly non-satiated, Section 1. These include all standard convex preferences including: linear of partly linear, constant elasticity of substitution (CES), Cobb Douglas, Leontief preferences, strictly convex preferences with indifference surfaces which intersect the coordinate lines or not and which contain half lines or not.

17. Or expectations.

18. As is done in finite dimensions. The Hahn-Banach theorem requires that one of the convex sets being separated has a non-empty interior.

19. See, e.g., [**15**] and more recently [**38**].

20. See also [**28**] and [**29**].

21. Called the Pareto frontier. The connection between limited arbitrage and the compactness of the Pareto frontier is of central importance for resource allocation. This connection was first pointed out and established in [**11, 13, 19, 22**] and [**28, 29**].

22. $R_+^N = \{(x_1, ..., x_N) \in R^N : \forall i, x_i \geq 0\}$.

23. If $x, y \in R^N$, $x \geq y \Leftrightarrow \forall i \ x_i \geq y_i$; $x > y \Leftrightarrow x \geq y$ and for some $i, x_i > y_i$; and $x >> y \Leftrightarrow \forall i, x_i > y_i$.

24. Namely independent of the utility representations.

25. This means that if $x \in \partial R_+^N$ and $u(x) > 0$, then $Du(x)$ is not orthogonal to ∂R_+^N at λx, $\forall \lambda \geq 0$. This condition includes strictly convex preferences, Cobb Douglas and CES preferences, many Leontief preferences $u(x, y) = \min(ax, by)$, preferences which are indifferent to one or more commodities, such as $u(x, y, z) = \sqrt{x + y}$, preferences with indifference surfaces which contain rays of ∂R_+^N such as $u(x, y, z) = x$, and preferences defined on a neighborhood of the positive orthant or the whole space, and which are increasing along the boundaries, e.g. $u(x, y, z) = x + y + z$.

26. Smoothness is used to simplify notation only: uniform non satiation requires no smoothness. This is a generalized Liftschitz condition: when preferences admit no smooth utility representation, then one requires $\exists \varepsilon, K > 0$: $\forall x, y \in X$ $K \parallel x - y \parallel > |$ and $\sup_{(y: \parallel x - y \parallel < a)} |u(x) - u(y)| > \varepsilon \parallel x - y \parallel$.

27. N is empty when $\forall h$, $\Omega_h \gg 0$.

28. The cone $A(\rho_h, \Omega_h)$ has points in common with Debreu's [31] "asymptotic cone" corresponding to the preferred set of u_h at the initial endowment Ω_h, in that along any of the rays of $A_h(\Omega_h)$ utility increases. Under Assumption 1, its closure $\overline{A}(\Omega_h)$, equals the "recession" cone introduced by Rockafeller, but not generally: along the rays in $A(\Omega_h)$ utility increases beyond the utility level of any other vector in the space. This condition need not be satisfied by Debreu's asymptotic cones [31] or by Rockafeller's "recession" cones. For example, for Leontief type preferences the recession cone through the endowment is the closure of the upper contour, which includes the indifference curve itself. By contrast, the cone $A_h(\Omega_h)$ is the interior of the upper contour set. Related concepts appeared in [6, 10]; otherwise there is no precedent in the literature for our cones. The cones used in the literature on no-arbitrage were Rockafeller's recession cones, until [11, 13] and [28].

29. See p. 85, (4).

30. The market cone D_h^+ is the whole consumption set $X = R^{N+}$ when $S(E)$ has a vector assigning strictly positive income to all individuals. If some trader has zero income, then this trader must have a boundary endowment.

31. A 'boundary ray' r in R_+^N consists of all the positive multiples of a vector $v \in \partial R_+^N$: $r = \{w \in R_+^N : \exists \lambda > 0 \text{ s.t. } w = \lambda v\}$

32. This includes Cobb-Douglas, constant elasticity of substitution (CES), preferences with indifference surfaces of positive consumption contained in the interior of R_+^N, linear preferences, piecewise linear preferences, most Leontief preferences, preferences with indifference surfaces which intersect the boundary of the positive orthant [2] and smooth utilities defined on a neighborhood of X which are transversal to its boundary ∂X.

33. The expression $G(\mathsf{E}) < \infty$ holds when $\forall h$, $\sup_{\{x : x \in X\}} u_h(x) = \infty$ as is assumed here; it must be replaced by $G(\mathsf{E}) < \sup_{\{x : x \in X^H : \sum x_h = \Omega\}} \left(\sum_{h=1}^H u_h(x_h) - u_h(\Omega_h) \right) - k$, for some positive k, when $\sup_{\{x : x \in X\}} u_h(x) < \infty$.

34. Z^c denotes the complement of the set Z.

35. A standard example of this phenomenon is in $L_\infty = \{f : R \to R : \sup_{x \in R} \|f(x)\| < \infty\}$. Society's endowment is $\Omega = (1,1,...,1,...)$, trader one has a preference $u_1(x) = \sup(x_i)$, and trader two has a preference $u_2(x) = \sum_i u(x_i)\lambda^{-i}$, $0 < \lambda < 1$. Then giving one more unit of the ith good to trader two always increases trader two's utility without decreasing that of trader one, and the Pareto frontier cannot be closed, see [29].

36. Recall that the Pareto frontier is defined as the set of individually rational, feasible and efficient utility allocations, see Section 1.2.

37. A set $X \subset H$ is bounded below when there exists $y \in H : \forall x \in H, x \geq y$.

38. A topological space X is homeomorphic to another Y when there exists an onto map $f : X \to Y$ which is continuous and has a continuous inverse.

39. The results on equilibrium in this paper originated from a theorem in [29] a paper which was submitted for publication in 1984, nine years before it appeared in print: these dates are recorded in the printed version. Chichilnisky and Heal in [30, 29] provided a no-arbitrage condition and proved it is sufficient for the existence of a competitive equilibrium with or without short sales, with infinitely or finitely many markets. See also the following footnote.

40. Chichilnisky and Heal in [30, 29], and [35], [34] and [46] among others, have defined various no-arbitrage conditions which they prove, under certain conditions on preferences, to be sufficient for existence of an equilibrium in different models. Except for [30, 29], none of these no-arbitrage conditions is generally necessary for existence. Within economies with short sales (which exclude Arrow Debreu's markets), and where preferences have no halflines in the indifference surfaces (which exclude "flats"), Werner [46] remarks (p. 1410, last para.) that another related condition (p. 1410, line -3) is necessary for existence, without however providing a complete proof of the equivalence between the condition which is necessary and that which is sufficient. In general, however, the two conditions in [46] are defined on different sets of cones: the sufficient condition is defined on cones S_i (p. 1410, line -14) while the necessary condition is defined on other cones, D_i (p. 1410, -3). The equivalence between the two cones depends on properties of yet another family of cones W_i (see p. 1410, lines 13-4). The definition of W_i on page 1408, line -15 shows that W_i is different from the recession cone R_i, (which are uniform by assumption) and therefore the cone W_i need not be uniform even when the recession cones are, as needed in Werner's Proposition 2. His argument for necessity is however complete in

a very special case: when preferences have uniform recession cones, the recession cones coincide with directions of strict utility increase and indifferences have no half lines: all these conditions are explicitly required throughout so that Werner's proof covers necessity for the economies in their 1994 paper. In general, however, even for the special case of economies with short sales and with strictly convex preferences, [11, 13, 18] and [22] and the results presented here appear to provide the first complete proof of a condition (limited arbitrage) which is simultaneously necessary and sufficient for the existence of a competitive equilibrium.

41. The no-arbitrage conditions in [29] and [46] do not provide necessary and sufficient conditions for all the economies considered in this paper: all prior results (except for those in [11, 13, 18, 22] depend crucially on the fact that the set of feasible allocations is compact. By contrast, the boundedness of feasible allocations is neither required, nor it is generally satisfied, in the economies considered in this paper, because although the feasible allocations may be unbounded, there exists a bounded set of allocations which reach all possible feasible utility levels.

42. A pseudoequilibrium, also called quasiequilibrium, is an allocation which clears the market and a price vector at which traders minimize cost within the utility levels achieved at their respective allocations. The connection between limited arbitrage and quasiequilibrium is studied in [24]. For the proof of existence of a quasiequilibrium, cf., [43], who studied the case where the economy has no short sales. For cases where short sales are allowed, and therefore feasible allocations may be unbounded, a method similar to Negishi's can be used, see, e.g., [30, 29] and [11, 13, 18, 22]. With strictly convex preferences, limited arbitrage implies that feasible allocations form a bounded set; otherwise, when indifferences have "flats", the set of feasible allocations may be unbounded. However in this latter case there exists a bounded set of feasible allocations which achieves all feasible utility levels, and this suffices for a Negishi-type proof of existence to go through.

43. Also known in subsequent work as "properness", see [14] and [38].

44. I proved this result in the finite dimensional case while at Stanford University in the Spring and Summer of 1993, stimulated by conversations with Curtis Eaves, and presented this result and its proof at the January 3-5, 1994 Meetings of the Econometric Society in Boston.

45. In the economy E the traders' preferences are defined over private consumption $u_i : R^N \to R$, but they define automatically preferences over allocations in $R^{N \times H}$: $u_i(x_1...x_H) \geq u_i(y_1...y_H) \Leftrightarrow u_i(x_i) \geq u_i(y_i)$.

46. See also [9].

47. A space X is contractible when there exists a continuous map $f : X \times [0,1] \to X$ and $x_o \in X$ such that $\forall x, f(x,0) = x$ and $f(x,1) = x_o$.

48. The concept of "large utility values" is purely ordinal; it is defined relative to the maximum utility value achieved by a utility representation.

49. If indifferences are bounded below, nothing is required of the sets of gradients. These conditions can be removed, but at the cost of more notation.

50. Recall that we have assumed, without loss, that $\sup_{x \in X} u_h(x) = \infty$. Otherwise the same statement holds by replacing "$> k$" by "$> \sup_{x \in X} u_h(x) - k$."

51. T could be the space of linear preferences on R^N or the space of strictly convex preferences on R^N, or the space of all smooth preferences. T could be endowed with the closed convergence topology, or the smooth topology, or the order topology, etc. T must satisfy a minimal regularity condition, for example to be locally convex (every point has a convex neighborhood) or, more generally, to be a parafinite CW complex. This is a very general specification, and includes all the spaces used routinely in economics, finite or infinite dimensional, such as all euclidean spaces, Banach and Hilbert spaces, manifolds, all piecewise linear spaces, polyhedrons, simplicial complexes, or finite or infinite dimensional CW spaces.

52. Since we apply Theorem 11, we require that the space of preferences P_J be connected. In a market economy, this requires that every two traders have a reason to trade, but says nothing about sets of three or more traders, nor does it imply limited arbitrage.

53. $\forall i, V_i \subset R^M$.

54. With integer coefficients.

55. Not all Arrow-Debreu exchange economies have a competitive equilibrium, even when all individual preferences are smooth, concave and increasing, and the consumption sets are positive orthants, $X = R_+^N$, see, for example, [2], Chapter 4, p. 80.

56. The results on existence of an equilibrium in [30, 29] (which are valid in finite or infinite dimensional economies) contain as a special case the results on existence of equilibrium in [46]. The no-arbitrage Condition C introduced by [30, 29] is weaker that the no-arbitrage condition defined by [46]. As recorded in its printed version, [29] was submitted for publication in February 1984. As recorded in its printed version, Werner's paper [46] was submitted for publication subsequently, in July 1985

References

[1] Arrow, K. [1951], *Social Choice and Individual Values*, Cowles Foundation Monograph, John Wiley and Sons, New York.

[2] Arrow, K. and Hahn, F. [1971], *General Competitive Analysis*, North Holland, San Francisco and New York. 1986.

[3] Arrow, K. and Debreu, G. [1954], *Existence of an Equilibrium for a Competitive Economy*, Econometrica **22**, 264-90.

[4] Baryshnikov, Y. [1993], *Unifying Impossibility Theorems: A Topological Approach*, Advances in Applied Mathematics **14**, 404-415.

[5] Black, D. [1948], *The Decisions of a Committee using a Simple Majority*, Econometrica **16**, 245-61.

[6] Chichilnisky, G. [1976], *Manifolds of Preferences and Equilibria*, Ph.D. Dissertation, Department of Economics, University of California, Berkeley, USA, published as Discussion Paper of the Project on Efficiency of Decision Making in Economic Systems, Harvard Univeristy, Cambridge, MA.

[7] Chichilnisky, G. [1980], *Social Choice and the Topology of Spaces of Preferences*, Advances in Mathematics **37**, No. 2, 165-176.

[8] Chichilnisky, G. [1980], *Intersecting Families of Sets*, Essex Economic Papers, University of Essex, U.K.

[9] Chichilnisky, G. [1982], *Social Aggregation Rules and Continuity*, Quarterly Journal of Economics, Vol. XCVII, 337-352.

[10] Chichilnisky, G. [1986], *Topological Complexity of Manifolds of Preferences*, in Essays in Honor of Gerard Debreu (W. Hildenbrand and A. Mas-Colell, eds.), North-Holland, New York, Chapter 8, pp. 131-142.

[11] Chichilnisky, G. [1991], *Markets, Arbitrage and Social Choice*, paper presented at the conference 'Columbia Celebrates Arrow's Contributions' Columbia University, New York, October 27, 1991, Working Paper No. 586, Columbia University, December 1992, and CORE Discussion Paper No. 9342, CORE, Universite Catolique de Louvain, Louvain la Neuve, Belgium, 1993.

[12] Chichilnisky, G. [1991], *Market Arbitrage, Social Choice and the Core*, Working paper, Columbia University, Social Choice and Welfare, (1997) **14**, 161-198.

[13] Chichilnisky, G. [1992], *Limited Arbitrage is Necessary and Sufficient for the Existence of a Competitive Equilibrium*, Working Paper No. 650, Columbia University Department of Economics, December 1992.

[14] Chichilnisky, G. [1993], *On Strategic Control*, Quarterly Journal of Economics **108**, 285-290.

[15] Chichilnisky, G. [1993], *The Cone Condition, Properness and Extremely Desirable Commodities*, Economic Theory **3**, 177-82.

[16] Chichilnisky, G. [1993], *Topology and Economics: the Contribution of Stephen Smale*, in From Topology to Computation (M. Hirsch, J. Marsden, and M. Shub, eds.), Proceedings of the Smalefest, Springer Verlag, New York-Heidelberg, pp. 147-161.

[17] Chichilnisky, G. [1993], *Intersecting Families of Sets and the Topology of Cones in Economics*, Bulletin of the American Mathematical Society, **29**, No. 2, pp. 189-207. First circulated as Essex Economic Papers, University of Essex, 1980.

[18] Chichilnisky, G. [1994], *Markets and Games: A simple equivalence among the core, equilibrium and limited arbitrage*, Metroeconomica, Vol. 47, October 1996, No. 3, p. 266-280.

[19] Chichilnisky, G. [1996], *Limited Arbitrage is Necessary and Sufficient for the Nonemptiness of the Core*, Economic Letters, August-September 1996 **52**, p. 177-180, Presented and distributed at the Yearly Meetings of the American Economic Association, Boston, January 3-5, 1994, previously published as *Limited Arbitrage is Necessary and Sufficient for the*

Existence of a Competitive Equilibrium and the Core and it Limits Voting Cycles, Economic Letters **46**, (1994), , pp. 321-331 in an issue which was subsequently reprinted by the editor without this paper.

[20] Chichilnisky, G. [1994], *Limited Arbitrage, Gains from Trade and Social Diversity: A Unified Perspective on Resource Allocation*, Working Paper, Columbia University, American Economic Review **84**, No. 2, 427-434.

[21] Chichilnisky, G. [1998], *Mathematical Economics*, Volumes I, II and III, Edward Elgar: The International Library of Critical Writings in Economics, Cheltenham, UK, Northampton, MA, USA.

[22] Chichilnisky, G. [1995], *Limited Arbitrage is Necessary and Sufficient for the Existence of a Competitive Equilibrium With or Without Short Sales*, Working Paper, Columbia University, March 1991, Economic Theory **5**, No. 1, 79-108, January 1995.

[23] Chichilnisky, G. [1995], *A Unified Perspective on Resource Allocation: Limited Arbitrage is Necessary and Sufficient for the Existence of a Competitive Equilibrium, the Core and Social Choice*, CORE Discussion Paper No. 9527, Universite Catolique de Louvain, Louvain-la-Neuve, Belgium.

[24] Chichilnisky, G. [1997], *A Topological Invariant for Competitive Markets*, Journal of Mathematical Economics **28**, 445-469.

[25] Chichilnisky, G. [1998], *Topology and invertible maps*, Advances in Applied Mathematics **21**, 113-123.

[26] Chichilnisky, G. and Kalman P. J. [1980], *Application of Functional Analysis to the Efficient Allocation of Economic Resources*, Journal of Optimization Theory and Applications **30**, No. 1, 19-32.

[27] Chichilnisky, G. and Heal, G. M. [1983], *Necessary and Sufficient Conditions for a Resolution of the Social Choice Paradox*, Journal of Economic Theory **31**, No. 1, 68-87.

[28] Chichilnisky, G. and Heal, G. M. [1992], *Arbitrage and Equilibrium in Sobolev Spaces*, First Boston Working Paper, Columbia University, revised in February 1995 under the title: *Equilibrium and the Core with Finitely or Infinitely Many Markets: A Unified Approach*,

[29] Chichilnisky, G. and Heal, G. M. [1993], *Existence of a Competitive Equilibrium in Sobolev Spaces without Bounds on Short Sales*, IMA Preprint series No. 79, Institute for Mathematics and its Applications, University of Minnesota, Minneapolis, Minnesota, June 1984. Submitted for publication in February 28, 1984, Journal of Economic Theory, Vol. 59, No. 2, pp. 364-384.

[30] Chichilnisky, G. and Heal, G. M. [1998], *A unified treatment of finite and infinite economies: limited arbitrage is necessary and sufficient for the existence of equilibrium and the core*, Economic Theory **12**, 163-176.

[31] Debreu, G. [1959], *The Theory of Value*, Cowles Foundation Monograph, John Wiley, New York.

[32] Debreu, G. [1962], *New Concepts and Techniques in Equilibrium Analysis*, International Economic Review **3**, 257-73.

[32] Grandmont, J. M. [1982], *Temporary Equilibrium*, in Handbook of Mathematical Economics (K. Arrow and M. Intriligator, eds.), North Holland, New York.

[33] Green, J. [1973], *Temporary Equilibrium in a Sequential Trading Model with Spot and Futures Transactions*, Econometrica **41**, No. 6, 1103 - 23.

[34] Hammond, P. [1983], *Overlapping Expectations and Hart's Conditions for Equilibrium in a Securities Market*, Journal of Economic Theory **31**, 170-75.

[35] Hart, O. [1974], *Existence of Equilibrium in a Securities Model*, Journal of Economic Theory **9**, 293-311.

[36] Heal, G. M. [1983], *Contractibility and Public Decision Making*, in Social Choice and Welfare (Chapter 7), (P. Pattanaik and S. Salles, eds.), North Holland, New York.

[37] Kreps, D. [1981], *Arbitrage and Equilibrium in Economies with Infinitely Many Commodities*, Journal of Mathematical Economics **8**, 15-35.

[38] Le Van, A. [1996], *Complete Characterization of Yannelis-Zame and Chichilnisky-Kalman-Mas Colell properness conditions on preferences for separable concave functions defined on L_+^p and L^p*, Economic Theory **8**, No. 1, 155-166.

[39] Koutsougeras, L. [1993], *The core in two-stage games*, Working Paper, University of Illinois, Urbana, Illinois.

[40] McKenzie, L. [1959], *On the existence of a general equilibrium for competitive markets*, Econometrica **27**, 54-71.

[41] McKenzie, L. [1961], *On the Existence of General Equilbrium: Some Corrections*, Economet-
     rica **29**, 247-248.

[42] McKenzie, L. [1987], *General Equilibrium*, in General Equilibrium, The New Palgrave, (J.
     Eatwell, M. Milgate and P. Newman, eds.), Norton, New York.

[43] Negishi, T. [1960], *Welfare Economics and the Existence of an Equilibrium for a Competitive
     Economy*, Metroeconomica **2**, 92-97.

[44] Nielsen, L. [1989], *Asset Market Equilibrium with Short Selling*, Review of Economic Studies
     56, No. 187, 467-473.

[45] Spanier, E. [1979], *Algebraic Topology*, McGraw Hill, New York.

[46] Werner, J. [1987], *Arbitrage and the Existence of Competitive Equilibrium*, Econometrica **55**,
     No. 6, 1403-1418.

Fields Institute Communications
Volume **22**, 1999

American Options on Dividend-Paying Assets

Mark Broadie
Graduate School of Business
Columbia University
New York, NY 10027 USA
mnb2@columbia.edu

Jérôme Detemple
Sloan School of Management
MIT, Cambridge, Massachusetts 02142 USA
and
Faculty of Management
McGill University, Montreal, Canada H3A 1G5
and
Cirano, Montreal, Canada H3A 2A5
detemple@management.mcgill.ca

Abstract. We provide a comprehensive treatment of option pricing with particular emphasis on the valuation of American options on dividend-paying assets. We begin by reviewing valuation principles for European contingent claims in a financial market in which the underlying asset price follows an Itô process and the interest rate is stochastic. Then this analysis is extended to the valuation of American contingent claims. In particular, the early exercise premium and the delayed exercise premium representations of the American option price are presented. These results are specialized in the case of the standard market model, i.e., when the underlying asset price follows a geometric Brownian motion process and the interest rate is constant. American capped options with constant and growing caps are then analyzed. Valuation formulas are first provided for capped options on dividend-paying assets in the context of the standard market model. Previously unpublished results are then presented for capped options on nondividend-paying assets when the underlying asset price follows an Itô process with stochastic volatility and the cap's growth rate is an adapted stochastic process.

1991 *Mathematics Subject Classification.* 90B09.

This paper is partly based on class notes for a course on Advanced Financial Economics taught at the Sloan School of Management, MIT, by J. Detemple in Spring 1995. A preliminary version of the paper was presented at the conference on Geometry, Topology and Markets which took place at The Fields Institute, University of Waterloo in July, 1994. We would like to thank the conference participants for helpful comments and we are particularly grateful to Angel Serrat for his detailed comments on an earlier draft of the paper.

1.1 Introduction

Contingent claims are not new financial instruments. Contracts of this type have indeed been exchanged for several centuries among economic agents. These securities have, however, experienced unprecedented growth in the past twenty years or so, since the creation of the first organized options market, the Chicago Board of Options Exchange (CBOE). Since the opening of this market, the number and the types of options contracts have substantially increased. Today investors can trade foreign exchange options, futures contracts, index options, and bond options in organized markets. Additionally, theoretical and technological progress in the past ten years has made it possible to engineer contracts with new provisions designed to meet specific investment needs. Capped options, Asian options, shout options, and other types of exotic securities can now be purchased in the over-the-counter market or can be issued by firms with specific financing needs.

The valuation of derivative securities has been the object of a long quest. A model describing the random behavior of speculative asset prices was initially proposed in [3]. The development of a rigorous theory of option pricing, however, only dates back to the 1970's. Black and Scholes in [6] proposed a valuation formula for European options which is consistent with the absence of arbitrage opportunities in the financial market. This model and the underlying methodology are refined and extended in [37]. An equivalent approach based on an appropriately chosen "risk neutral" valuation operator was pioneered by [16]. The foundations and principles underlying these valuation methods are identified and characterized in the seminal paper [27].

The valuation of American options also has a long history. Samuelson in [42] and Mckean in [36] initially treat this problem as a stopping time problem unrelated to the pricing measure embedded in the underlying asset prices. It is only recently, however, that the optimal stopping problem has been posed relative to an appropriate measure which correctly prices American options ([5] and [32]). Karatzas in [32], in particular, shows that the American option payoff can be replicated by a carefully chosen strategy of investment in the primary assets in the model. The value of the American option, then, must equal the value of the replicating portfolio to avoid arbitrage opportunities and be consistent with economic equilibrium.

While the stopping time approach to American option valuation is instructive, it does not provide much insight into the properties of the optimal exercise boundary, nor does it lead to efficient numerical procedures. Authors in [34], [30] and [14] derive, in the context of the standard market model (geometric Brownian motion for the underlying asset price and a constant interest rate), an early exercise premium representation of the value of the American option. This representation expresses the value of the American option as the corresponding European option value plus the gains from early exercise. The gains from early exercise are the present value of the dividend benefits in the exercise region net of the interest losses on the payments incurred upon exercise.

In fact, the early exercise premium formula is the Riesz decomposition of the Snell envelope which arises in the stopping time problem associated with the valuation of the option contract. The Riesz decomposition was initially proved in the context of stopping time problems in [22]. Myneni in [38] adapts their results to the American put pricing problem in the context of the standard market model. The decomposition was recently extended to a fairly general class of market models with semimartingale price processes in [**41**].

The early exercise premium representation is written in terms of the optimal exercise boundary. By imposing a boundary condition, this representation can be used to derive a recursive integral equation for the optimal exercise boundary. This equation can be used in a numerical procedure to solve for the optimal exercise boundary which determines the value of the American option.

While the valuation of standard American option contracts has now achieved a fair degree of maturity, much work remains to be done regarding the new contractual forms that are constantly emerging in response to new economic conditions and regulations. One innovation which has received some attention is the class of capped option contracts. These are options with a ceiling on their payoff (or a floor for put options) which limits the potential gains from early exercise. These options are attractive from the perspective of issuers since they limit their potential liabilities, yet they retain some attractiveness for purchasers since they provide upside potential and are less costly than their uncapped counterpart. As a result, such options have appeared as components of securities issued by firms to cover certain financing needs. A recent treatment of these options, in the context of the standard market model, appears in [**10**].

In this paper we provide a comprehensive treatment of option pricing with particular emphasis on the valuation of American options on dividend-paying assets. In the second section we review valuation principles for European contingent claims in a financial market in which the underlying asset price follows an Itô process and the interest rate is stochastic. In Section 1.3 the analysis is extended to American contingent claims. In this context we review the basic valuation principle for American options. We also provide two representation formulas, the early exercise premium and the delayed exercise premium representations, which are based on recent developments in the field. These results are then applied in Section 1.4 to American option valuation in the context of the standard market model, i.e., when the underlying asset price follows a geometric Brownian motion process and the interest rate is constant. American capped options with constant and growing caps are analyzed in Section 1.5. Valuation formulas are first provided for capped options on dividend-paying assets in the context of the standard market model. Previously unpublished results are then presented for capped options on nondividend-paying assets when the underlying asset price follows an Itô process with stochastic volatility and the cap's growth rate is an adapted stochastic process.

1.2 The valuation of European contingent claims

We first define the classes of contingent claims which are the focus of our analysis (subsection 1.2.1). We proceed with a description of the economic setting (subsection 1.2.2). Attainable European contingent claims are then characterized (subsection 1.2.3) and valued (subsection 1.2.4).

1.2.1 Definitions

A *derivative security* is a financial contract whose payoff depends on the price(s) of some underlying or *primary* asset(s). In their most general form, derivative securities generate a flow of payments over periods of time as well as cash payments at specific dates. In addition, the cash flows need not be paid at fixed points in time or during fixed periods of time. Some derivative securities involve cash flows paid at prespecified random times or even at (random) times which are chosen by the holder of the contract.

The standard example of a derivative security is an *option* contract. An option gives the holder of the contract the right, but not the obligation, to buy (or sell) a given asset, at a predetermined price (the *exercise* or *strike* price), at or before some prespecified future date (the maturity date). The option to buy (sell) is a *call* (*put*) option. A *European* option contract can be exercised at the fixed maturity date T only. Since exercise at maturity is only optimal if the option is in the money, the payoff on a European call option written on a stock equals $(S_T - K)^+$, where S_T is the price of the underlying stock (primary asset) at the specified maturity date and $K > 0$ is the exercise price of the contract. An *American* option contract can be exercised at any time at or before the maturity date.

1.2.2 The Economy

We consider an economy with the following characteristics. The uncertainty is represented by a complete probability space $(\Omega, \mathcal{F}, P)$ where Ω is the set of elementary events or "states of nature" with generic element ω, $\mathcal{F}$ is a σ-algebra representing the collection of observable events and P is a probability measure defined on $(\Omega, \mathcal{F})$. The time period is the finite interval $[0, T]$. A Brownian motion process z is defined on $(\Omega, \mathcal{F}, P)$ with values in the real numbers **R**. The flow of information is given by the natural filtration $\{\mathcal{F}_t\}$, i.e., the P-augmentation of the Brownian filtration. Without loss of generality we set $\mathcal{F}_T = \mathcal{F}$ so that all the observable events are eventually known. Our model for information and beliefs is $(\Omega, \mathcal{F}, \{\mathcal{F}_t, t \in [0, T]\}, P)$.

Two types of financial securities are traded in the asset market: a riskless asset (bond) and a risky asset (stock). The price of the riskless asset, B, satisfies the equation

$$dB_t = r_t B_t dt, t \in [0, T], \ B_0 \text{ given}, \tag{1.2.1}$$

where $r = \{r_t, \mathcal{F}_t : t \in [0, T]\}$ is a bounded, strictly positive and progressively measurable process of the filtration which represents the interest rate in the economy. For notational convenience, define the discount factor $R_{s,t} = \exp(-\int_s^t r_v dv)$.

The price of the stock satisfies the stochastic differential equation

$$dS_t = S_t[(\mu_t - \delta_t)dt + \sigma_t dz_t], t \in [0, T], \ S_0 \text{ given}. \tag{1.2.2}$$

The process $\delta \equiv \{\delta_t, \mathcal{F}_t : t \in [0, T]\}$ represents the dividend rate on the stock; $\mu \equiv \{\mu_t, \mathcal{F}_t : t \in [0, T]\}$ and $\sigma \equiv \{\sigma_t, \mathcal{F}_t : t \in [0, T]\}$ are the drift and the volatility coefficients of the stock's total rate of return, respectively. The coefficients δ, μ, and σ are bounded and progressively measurable processes of the filtration. The dividend rate is nonnegative, $\delta \geq 0$; the volatility σ is bounded above and bounded away from zero (P-a.s.), i.e., the financial market under consideration is complete.

Remark 1.2.1 The financial market is *complete* when a relevant class of state contingent claims, i.e., cash flows that depend on the realized trajectories of the Brownian motion process z, can be attained by an appropriate portfolio of available financial assets. When the volatility coefficient σ is bounded away from zero, the stochastic shocks affecting the financial market (the Brownian motion z) can be hedged away, at all times, by investing in the stock. The ability to design unconstrained investment strategies in the stock and in the bond, then, ensures the attainability of these contingent claims ([**27**], [**28**], [**19**]).

It has become standard to use stochastic processes of the form (1.2.2) to model the behavior of stock prices. For instance, the geometric Brownian motion process which is obtained by taking constant coefficients (μ, σ, δ), is used as a basis for the analysis in [**6**]. Alternative formulations which have received attention include some processes with jumps ([**37**], [**16**]).

In order to determine the prices of contingent claims we start by characterizing the set of random variables (payoffs) that can be generated by trading strategies involving only the stock and the bond.

Let X denote the wealth process generated by an investment strategy in the financial assets (1.2.1)–(1.2.2). We first define the set of "allowable" or "admissible" consumption-investment strategies. A portfolio process $\pi = \{\pi_t, \mathcal{F}_t : t \in [0, T]\}$ is a progressively measurable, $\mathbf{R}$-valued process such that $\int_0^T \pi_t dt < \infty$, (P-a.s.). Here π_t denotes the (dollar) investment in the stock at date t; the amount invested in the bond contract is $X_t - \pi_t$. A cumulative consumption process $C = \{C_t, \mathcal{F}_t : t \in [0, T]\}$ is a progressively measurable, nondecreasing, right-continuous process with values in $\mathbf{R}$ and initial value $C_0 = 0$. Since we consider nondecreasing cumulative consumption processes only, the portfolio processes under consideration allow for withdrawal of funds (for consumption purposes). When cumulative consumption is null at all times the portfolio is said to be self-financing: it involves neither infusions nor withdrawals of funds but only rebalancing of the existing positions held in the different assets.

An investment of π_t in the stock at date t produces a total return (capital gains plus dividends) equal to $\pi_t[(dS_t/S_t) + \delta_t dt]$. An investment of $X_t - \pi_t$ in the bond has a return of $(X_t - \pi_t)r_t dt$. The activity of consumption reduces wealth by the corresponding amount dC_t. Hence, a consumption-portfolio strategy (C, π) generates the wealth process X which solves the stochastic differential equation

$$
\begin{aligned}
dX_t &= (X_t - \pi_t)r_t dt + \pi_t[(dS_t/S_t) + \delta_t dt] - dC_t, t \in [0, T]; X_0 = x, \\
&= r_t X_t dt + \pi_t(\mu_t - r_t)dt + \pi_t \sigma_t dz_t - dC_t, t \in [0, T]; X_0 = x.
\end{aligned}
\tag{1.2.3}
$$

Given an initial investment $x > 0$, a consumption-portfolio strategy (C, π) is *admissible*, if the associated wealth process X solving (1.2.3) satisfies the nonnegativity constraint

$$
X_t \geq 0, \quad t \in [0, T] \quad \text{(P-a.s.)} \tag{1.2.4}
$$

This condition is a no-bankruptcy condition which stipulates that wealth cannot be negative during the trading period. Let $\mathcal{A}(x)$ denote the set of admissible strategies.

A European contingent claim (f, Y) is composed of a cumulative payment process $f \equiv \{f_t, \mathcal{F}_t : t \in [0, T]\}$ which is nondecreasing, progressively measurable, right-continuous and null at zero, and a nonnegative $\mathcal{F}_T$-measurable cash flow Y at date T.

A consumption-portfolio strategy (C, π) *generates* a European contingent claim (f, Y) if (C, π) is admissible, $C_t = f_t$, and $X_T = Y$. The claim (f, Y) is *attainable* from an initial investment x if there exists an admissible consumption-portfolio strategy such that $dC_t \geq df_t$ for all $t \in [0, T]$ and $X_T \geq Y$ (P-a.s.).

1.2.3 Attainable Contingent Claims

The pricing of contingent claims amounts to the identification of an appropriate valuation operator which maps future payoffs into current prices. Since the processes satisfying (1.2.1) and (1.2.2) represent the prices of traded assets, this valuation operator must be consistent with these prices. In fact, as will become clear below, the price processes (1.2.1)–(1.2.2) completely determine the valuation operator in this economy.

The market model (1.2.1) and (1.2.2) implies a unique market price per unit risk $\theta \equiv \{\theta_t, \mathcal{F}_t : t \in [0,T]\}$ equal to $\theta_t = \sigma_t^{-1}(\mu_t - r_t)$. This one-dimensional process is well defined, progressively measurable and bounded since σ is bounded away from zero; it is uniquely defined because of market completeness. The market price of risk represents the excess expected return implicitly assigned by the model (1.2.1)–(1.2.2) to the stochastic shocks z affecting the financial market.

Consider now the exponential process $\eta \equiv \{\eta_t, \mathcal{F}_t : t \in [0,T]\}$ defined by

$$\eta_t = e^{-\left(\int_0^t \theta_s dz_s + \frac{1}{2}\int_0^t \theta_s^2 ds\right)}. \tag{1.2.5}$$

Boundedness of the market price of risk implies that the Novikov condition is satisfied; it follows that η is a martingale ([33], Chapter 3, Corollary 5.13). We can then define the *equivalent martingale probability measure*, $Q(A) = E[\eta_T \mathbf{1}_A]$, $A \in \mathcal{F}_T$. That is, Q is equivalent to P and is unique due to the completeness of the financial market. Additionally, by the Girsanov Theorem ([33], Chapter 3, Theorem 5.1) the process $\tilde{z}_t = z_t + \int_0^t \theta_s ds$, for $t \in [0,T]$, is a standard Q-Brownian motion process.

Under the equivalent martingale measure Q, the ex-dividend price process $R_{0,t} S_t$ is a Q-supermartingale (recall $R_{s,t} \equiv \exp(-\int_s^t r_v dv)$). The process consisting of the discounted ex-dividend price augmented by the discounted dividends, $S_t^* \equiv R_{0,t} S_t + \int_0^t R_{0,v} \delta_v S_v dv$, is a Q-martingale. It satisfies the equation

$$dS_t^* = R_{0,t} S_t \sigma_t d\tilde{z}_t, t \in [0,T]; S_0^* = S_0. \tag{1.2.6}$$

We conclude that the *present value* formula

$$S_t = E^*\left[R_{t,T} S_T + \int_t^T R_{t,v} \delta_v S_v dv | \mathcal{F}_t\right] \tag{1.2.7}$$

holds, where E^* denotes the expectation relative to the measure Q. In this formula the discount rate is locally riskless (conditional on contemporaneous information) but risky relative to the information available strictly prior to current time. Hence the discount factor $R_{t,T}$ is an $\mathcal{F}_T$-measurable random variable which cannot be factored out of the expectation operator $E^*[\cdot | \mathcal{F}_t]$. Finally, we note that the system of Arrow-Debreu prices implied by the price system (1.2.1)–(1.2.2) is given by $R_{0,t} \eta_t dP$: these prices represent the value attributed by the market at date 0 to one dollar paid in state (t, ω). The *state price density* is defined as $\xi_t \equiv R_{0,t} \eta_t$.

Consider European contingent claims (f, Y) which satisfy the integrability condition

$$E[\xi_T Y] + E\left[\int_0^T \xi_s df_s\right] < \infty. \tag{1.2.8}$$

Let I denote this class of claims.

Our first theorem provides a characterization of the set of attainable contingent claims.

Theorem 1.2.2 *Consider a contingent claim $(f, Y) \in I$. If (f, Y) is attainable at date T from an initial investment x then*

$$E^*[R_{0,T} Y] + E^*\left[\int_0^T R_{0,s} df_s\right] \leq x. \tag{1.2.9}$$

Equivalently, if (f, Y) is attainable from x then

$$E[\eta_T R_{0,T} Y] + E\left[\int_0^T \eta_s R_{0,s} df_s\right] \leq x$$

where the expectation is taken relative to the measure P. Conversely, suppose that (1.2.9) holds. Then there exists an admissible consumption-portfolio strategy (C, π) such that (f, Y) is attainable from the initial wealth x.

In Proposition 1.2.6 below we show that $E^*[R_{0,T} Y] + E^*[\int_0^T R_{0,s} df_s]$ represents the present value at date 0 of the contingent claim (f, Y). Hence, the condition (1.2.9) states that the present value of the contingent claim (f, Y) is less than or equal to the value of initial wealth x which attains the claim.

Proof of Theorem 1.2.2 (i) Necessity: consider an admissible policy $(C, \pi) \in \mathcal{A}(x)$. The associated wealth process corresponding to an initial investment x is the solution to equation (1.2.3) given by

$$X_t = R_{0,t}^{-1}\left(x - \int_0^t R_{0,s} dC_s + \int_0^t R_{0,s}\pi_{1s}(\mu_s - r_s)ds + \int_0^t R_{0,s}\pi_s\sigma_s dz_s\right) \quad (1.2.10)$$

for all $t \in [0, T]$. Equivalently, using the definition of the process $\tilde{z}$,

$$X_t R_{0,t} + \int_0^t R_{0,s} dC_s = x + \int_0^t R_{0,s}\pi_{1s}\sigma_s d\tilde{z}_s. \quad (1.2.11)$$

The right-hand side of (1.2.11) is a continuous Q-local martingale. Admissibility of (C, π) implies that the left-hand side of (1.2.11) is nonnegative. The combination of these two properties implies that the right-hand side is a nonnegative Q-supermartingale ([**33**], Chapter 1, Problem 5.19). Taking expectations on both sides of (1.2.11) and setting $t = T$ yields

$$E^*[R_{0,T} X_T] + E^*\left[\int_0^T R_{0,s} dC_s\right] \leq x. \quad (1.2.12)$$

Hence if (f, Y) is attainable ($X_T \geq Y$ and $dC_t \geq df_t$ for all $t \in [0, T]$) from initial wealth x then

$$E^*[R_{0,T} Y] + E^*\left[\int_0^T R_{0,s} df_s\right] \leq E^*[R_{0,T} X_T] + E^*\left[\int_0^T R_{0,s} dC_s\right] = x \quad (1.2.13)$$

and (1.2.9) follows.

(ii) Sufficiency: conversely, suppose that $(f, Y) \in I$ satisfies Equation (1.2.9). By the fundamental representation theorem for Brownian martingales ([**33**], Chapter 3, Theorem 4.15) the P-martingale M_t defined by

$$E[\eta_T R_{0,T} Y | \mathcal{F}_t] + E\left[\eta_T \int_0^T R_{0,s} df_s | \mathcal{F}_t\right]$$

has the representation

$$M_t = M_0 + \int_0^t \phi_s dz_s \quad (1.2.14)$$

where $\phi \equiv \{\phi_t, \mathcal{F}_t : t \in [0, T]\}$ is a one-dimensional, $\mathcal{F}_t$-progressively measurable process such that $\int_0^T \phi_t^2 dt < \infty$ (P-a.s.). An application of Bayes' law shows that the Q-martingale $M_t^* \equiv E^*[R_{0,T}Y|\mathcal{F}_t] + E^*[\int_0^T R_{0,s}df_s|\mathcal{F}_t]$ equals

$$M_t^* = \eta_t^{-1} M_t.$$

Using (1.2.5), (1.2.14), and applying Itô's lemma leads to $M_t^* = M_0^* + \int_0^t \phi_s^* d\tilde{z}_s$, where $\phi_t^* \equiv \eta_t^{-1}(\phi_t + M_t\theta_t)$ and $\tilde{z}$ is the Q-Brownian motion process defined earlier. Selecting the portfolio process $\pi_t = R_{0,t}^{-1}\sigma_t^{-1}\phi_t^*$ and replacing in the wealth process X of Equation (1.2.11) yields

$$R_{0,t}X_t + \int_0^t R_{0,s}dC_s = x + \int_0^t \phi_s^* d\tilde{z}_s$$

$$= x - E^*\left[R_{0,T}Y + \int_0^T R_{0,s}df_s\right] + E^*\left[R_{0,T}Y + \int_0^T R_{0,s}df_s|\mathcal{F}_t\right],$$

$$\tag{1.2.15}$$

for $t \in [0, T]$. At time T we get $R_{0,T}X_T + \int_0^T R_{0,s}dC_s = x - E^*[R_{0,T}Y + \int_0^T R_{0,s}df_s] + (R_{0,T}Y + \int_0^T R_{0,s}df_s)$ since $R_{0,T}Y + \int_0^T R_{0,s}df_s$ is $\mathcal{F}_T$-measurable. Condition (1.2.9) then implies $R_{0,T}X_T + \int_0^T R_{0,s}dC_s \geq R_{0,T}Y + \int_0^T R_{0,s}df_s$. Selecting $C = f$ yields $X_T \geq Y$. Furthermore $X_T = Y$ (P-a.s.) if (1.2.9) holds with equality.

Remark 1.2.3 As shown in the sufficiency part of Theorem 1.2.2, the wealth process associated with the consumption-portfolio strategy (C, π) that generates (f, Y) is

$$X_t = E^*\left[R_{t,T}Y + \int_t^T R_{t,s}df_s|\mathcal{F}_s\right], \quad t \in [0, T].$$

Hence the wealth process is nonnegative at all times, since f and Y are nonnegative. The wealth process equals the present value of the future cash flows generated by the policy (C, π).

1.2.4 The Valuation of Attainable Contingent Claims

Given our characterization of attainable contingent claims in Theorem 1.2.2 it is now easy to deduce their market value. To this end, we define the notion of an *arbitrage* opportunity and the *rational price* of a contingent claim. Suppose that the claim (f, y) is marketed at some price V. Agents can now invest in the stock, the riskless asset and in the contingent claim. Let π_f denote the investment in the claim.

Definition 1.2.4 *A consumption-portfolio strategy (C, π, π_f) is an arbitrage opportunity if $(C, \pi, \pi_f) \in \mathcal{A}(0)$, $P(X_T \geq 0) = 1$, and $P(X_T > 0) > 0$.*

An arbitrage opportunity is a consumption-portfolio strategy which has zero initial cost, requires no intermediate cash infusions, and has a strictly positive probability of positive wealth at time T (and zero probability of negative wealth).

Definition 1.2.5 *The rational price of the claim (f, Y) is the price which is consistent with the absence of arbitrage opportunities in the financial market.*

The rational price of the contingent claim (f, Y) is also called the *market value* of the claim. Indeed, deviations of the market price from the rational price would lead to infinite demand for the arbitrage portfolio. This situation is inconsistent with an equilibrium in the financial market at these prices. Since the financial market is complete, the rational price of an attainable contingent claim is unique. We are now ready to provide a valuation formula for the contingent claim.

Proposition 1.2.6 *The rational price at time t of the European contingent claim $(f, Y) \in I$ is uniquely given by*

$$V_t(f, Y) = E^*[R_{t,T}Y|\mathcal{F}_t] + E^* \left[\int_t^T R_{t,s} df_s | \mathcal{F}_t \right]$$

for $t \in [0, T]$.

Proof of Proposition 1.2.6 The contingent claim (f, Y) is attainable from all initial investments x satisfying the budget constraint (1.2.9). Minimizing over this set yields the (unique) minimum investment from which (f, Y) is attainable: $x^* = E^*[R_{0,T}Y] + E^*[\int_0^T R_{0,s} df_s]$. The rational price of Y at date zero must then equal $V_0(f, Y) = x^*$ for otherwise an arbitrage opportunity exists. Since the sum of discounted wealth plus cumulative discounted dividends is a Q-martingale, similar reasoning establishes that the minimum amount of wealth that must be invested at date t to generate (f, Y) is $X_t = E^*[R_{t,T}Y|\mathcal{F}_t] + E^*[\int_t^T R_{t,s} df_s | \mathcal{F}_t]$. The price of the claim at date t follows.

Proposition 1.2.6 provides our most general pricing formula in the context of the Itô financial market model (1.2.1)–(1.2.2). It states that the value of any European contingent claim involving cash flow payments over $[0, T]$ is simply the expected value of the discounted cash flows. Here discounting is made at the locally riskfree interest rate whereas the expectation is taken under the equivalent martingale measure implicit in the market model (1.2.1)–(1.2.2). Note that this present value formula is valid even though the riskfree rate as well as the drift and volatility of the stock price process are progressively measurable processes of the Brownian filtration, i.e., even though they may depend on the history of the Brownian motion. If the market price of the contingent claim ever deviates from the rational price prescribed by the formula, it is possible to construct a portfolio of the claim, the stock, and the bond, and a trading strategy which represents an arbitrage opportunity.

Standard European option contracts involve a payment at the maturity date T only. For a call option the cumulative payment flow is $f = 0$ and the terminal payoff is $Y = (S_T - K)^+$; for a put option $f = 0$ and $Y = (K - S_T)^+$. In these cases the pricing formula $V_t(f, Y)$ specializes as follows.

Corollary 1.2.7 *In the financial market model (1.2.1)–(1.2.2) the rational price of a European call option with maturity date T and exercise price K is given by $C_t = E^*[R_{t,T}(S_T - K)^+|\mathcal{F}_t]$, for $t \in [0, T]$. The price of a European put option is $P_t = E^*[R_{t,T}(K - S_T)^+|\mathcal{F}_t]$, for $t \in [0, T]$.*

When the interest rate is constant, the price of an option written on a nondividend-paying stock whose price follows a geometric Brownian motion process satisfies the formula by Black and Scholes [6] (see also [37]).

Corollary 1.2.8 ([6]) *Suppose that the interest rate r is constant and that the stock price follows a geometric Brownian motion process without dividends ((μ, σ) constants, $\delta = 0$). Then the price of a European call option simplifies to*

$$C_t = S_t N(d) - e^{-r\tau} K N(d - \sigma\sqrt{\tau}) \qquad (1.2.16)$$

where $\tau \equiv T - t$ is the time to maturity, $N(\cdot)$ is the cumulative standard normal distribution function, and $d \equiv (\sigma\sqrt{\tau})^{-1}(\log(S_t/K) + (r + \frac{1}{2}\sigma^2)\tau)$. The price of the associated European put option with same maturity and exercise price is obtained from the put-call parity relationship: $P_t = C_t - S_t + e^{-r\tau} K$.

Proof of Corollary 1.2.8 Under the conditions stated, Proposition 1.2.6 shows that the option price is given by $C_t = e^{-r\tau} E^*[(S_T - K)^+ | \mathcal{F}_t]$. Define the exercise region as the set $E \equiv \{\omega \in \Omega : S_T \geq K\}$ of states of nature in which the stock price at date T exceeds the exercise price K. Let $\mathbf{1}_E$ denote the indicator of E. Then the option price simplifies to $C_t = e^{-r\tau} E^*[\mathbf{1}_E(S_T - K)|\mathcal{F}_t] = e^{-r\tau}(E^*[\mathbf{1}_E S_T | \mathcal{F}_t] - K E^*[\mathbf{1}_E | \mathcal{F}_t])$. The second expectation appearing in this expression is simply the Q-measure of the set E conditional on the information at date t. Under the measure Q the stock price is given by $S_T = S_t e^{(r - \frac{1}{2}\sigma^2)\tau + \sigma(\tilde{z}_T - \tilde{z}_t)}$ where $\tilde{z}_T - \tilde{z}_t$ is distributionally equivalent to $\tilde{z}\sqrt{T - t}$ where the random variable $\tilde{z}$ follows has a normal distribution with mean zero and unit variance. It follows that

$$E^*[\mathbf{1}_E | \mathcal{F}_t] = Q(E; \mathcal{F}_t) = Q(\tilde{z}_T - \tilde{z}_t \geq \sigma^{-1}[\log(K/S_t) - (r - \frac{1}{2}\sigma^2)\tau])$$
$$= 1 - N(-d + \sigma\sqrt{\tau}) = N(d - \sigma\sqrt{\tau}), \qquad (1.2.17)$$

where $N(\cdot)$ is the cumulative standard normal distribution. The first expectation simplifies to

$$e^{-r\tau}[E^*[\mathbf{1}_E S_T | \mathcal{F}_t] = S_t E^*[\mathbf{1}_E e^{-\frac{1}{2}\sigma^2\tau + \sigma(\tilde{z}_T - \tilde{z}_t)} | \mathcal{F}_t]$$
$$= S_t \int_{-\infty}^{\infty} \mathbf{1}_E e^{-\frac{1}{2}\sigma^2\tau + \sigma u\sqrt{\tau}} n(u)du, \qquad (1.2.18)$$

where $n(u)$ is the density of the standard normal. Computing the integral yields formula (1.2.16).

To prove the put-call parity relationship, note that $(K - S_T)^+ = (S_T - K)^+ - S_T + K$. No arbitrage implies that the value of the put must equal the value of the portfolio of the securities on the right-hand side of the equality. The parity relationship follows.

An explicit formula for the option can also be computed when the coefficients of the model change deterministically over time.

Corollary 1.2.9 (Black-Scholes with deterministic coefficients) *Consider the financial market model with deterministic interest rate, drift and volatility coefficients (r_t, μ_t, σ_t) without dividends ($\delta = 0$). Then, the price of a European call option is given by*

$$C_t = S_t N(d) - R_{t,T} K N\left(d - \left(\int_t^T \sigma_v^2 dv\right)^{\frac{1}{2}}\right) \qquad (1.2.19)$$

where $N(\cdot)$ is the cumulative standard normal distribution function and

$$d \equiv \left(\int_t^T \sigma_v^2 dv \right)^{-\frac{1}{2}} \left[\log(S_t/K) + \int_t^T \left(r_v + \frac{1}{2}\sigma_v^2 \right) dv \right].$$

Proof of Corollary 1.2.9 Under the assumptions stated, the stock price S_T equals $S_t \exp(\int_t^T (r_v - \frac{1}{2}\sigma_v^2)dv + \int_t^T \sigma_v d\tilde{z}_v)$. Furthermore the stochastic integral $\int_t^T \sigma_v d\tilde{z}_v$ has normal distribution with zero mean and variance $\int_t^T \sigma_v^2 dv$. Performing the same computations as in the proof of Corollary 1.2.8 yields the result.

The next result provides the price of a European option on a dividend-paying stock in a financial market with deterministic coefficients.

Corollary 1.2.10 (Black-Scholes with dividend adjustment) *Consider the financial market model with deterministic interest rate, drift and volatility coefficients, and dividend rate $(r_t, \mu_t, \sigma_t, \delta_t)$, respectively. The price of a European call option is given by*

$$C_t = S_t D_{t,T} N(d) - R_{t,T} K N \left(d - \left(\int_t^T \sigma_v^2 dv \right)^{\frac{1}{2}} \right) \tag{1.2.20}$$

where $D_{t,T} \equiv \exp(-\int_t^T \delta_v dv)$, $N(\cdot)$ is the cumulative standard normal distribution function, and

$$d \equiv \left(\int_t^T \sigma_v^2 dv \right)^{-\frac{1}{2}} \left[\log(S_t/K) + \int_t^T \left(r_v - \delta_v + \frac{1}{2}\sigma_v^2 \right) dv \right].$$

1.3 American contingent claims

We now turn to the valuation of American contingent claims. These claims can be exercised during certain prespecified periods of time at the option of the holder of the security. To value these contracts we first need to identify the optimal exercise strategy. The absence of arbitrage opportunities implies that the value of the contract is its value under the optimal exercise policy.

In this section we provide three representations of the price of an American contingent claim. The results are used in the next two sections to provide explicit valuation formulas for standard American options and capped American options when the underlying asset price follows a geometric Brownian motion process.

As a preliminary step we extend the valuation formula in Proposition 1.2.6 to securities with payoffs at random times. The economic setting is the one described in subsection 1.2.2.

A random time τ is a *stopping time* of the (Brownian) filtration $\{\mathcal{F}_t : t \in [0, T]\}$ if the event $\{\tau \le t\}$ belongs to the σ-field $\mathcal{F}_t$ for every $t \in [0, T]$. That is, τ is a stopping time if an observer can tell, on the basis of his current information, whether τ has occurred before or at the current time t. Let $\mathcal{S}_{0,T}$ denote the set of stopping times taking values in $[0, T]$.

Consider a contingent claim (f, Y) and an exogenously specified stopping time $\tau \in \mathcal{S}_{0,T}$. Here $f \equiv \{f_t, \mathcal{F}_t : t \in [0, \tau]\}$ is a cumulative payment process prior to τ which is nondecreasing, progressively measurable, right-continuous and null at zero. Also Y is used to represent a nonnegative and progressively measurable process with value Y_τ at time τ. By analogy with Section 1.2 we consider (f, Y) which satisfy the integrability condition

$$E[\xi_\tau Y_\tau] + E\left[\int_0^\tau \xi_s df_s\right] < \infty, \tag{1.3.1}$$

for all $\tau \in \mathcal{S}_{0,T}$. Let IS denote this class of claims.

Theorem 1.3.1 *Let τ denote a stopping time in $\mathcal{S}_{0,T}$ and suppose that $(f, Y) \in IS$. The rational price of this contingent claim is uniquely given by*

$$E^*\left[\int_t^\tau R_{t,s} df_s | \mathcal{F}_t\right] + E^*[R_{t,\tau} Y_\tau | \mathcal{F}_t], \tag{1.3.2}$$

at any time $t \in [0, \tau]$.

If, instead of being exogenously specified, the stopping time τ can be chosen by the holder of the contingent claim, (f, Y) is an *American contingent claim*. Since this choice can only be based on the information available (and since information is assumed to be homogeneous among participants in the financial market) the exercise decision can be thought of as the selection of the best stopping time τ of the filtration with values in $[0, T]$. The next theorem shows that the value of the contract is the value under the best exercise policy.

Theorem 1.3.2 ([**5**], [**32**]) *Suppose that $(f, Y) \in IS$. Consider an American contingent claim (f, Y). The rational price $V_t(f, Y)$ of this claim is uniquely given by*

$$V_t(f, Y) = \sup_{\tau \in \mathcal{S}_{t,T}} \left(E^*\left[\int_t^\tau R_{t,s} df_s | \mathcal{F}_t\right] + E^*[R_{t,\tau} Y_\tau | \mathcal{F}_t]\right), \tag{1.3.3}$$

at time $t \in [0, T]$.

Proof of Theorem 1.3.2 We prove the theorem for the case $f = 0$. The proof follows [**32**]. For $t \in [0, T]$ define the discounted payoff process

$$D_t \equiv R_{0,t} Y_t.$$

From the theory of optimal stopping (see, for instance, [**21**]) we conclude that there exists a nonnegative, right-continuous with left-hand limits Q-supermartingale $Z \equiv \{Z_t, \mathcal{F}_t : t \in [0, T]\}$ such that

$$Z_t = \sup_{\tau \in \mathcal{S}_{t,T}} E^*[D_\tau | \mathcal{F}_t]$$

for all $t \in [0, T]$. The process Z is the *Snell envelope* of D. Furthermore, the optimal stopping time τ_t is given by

$$\tau_t \equiv \inf\{s \in [t, T] : Z_s = D_s\}. \tag{1.3.4}$$

In order to show that (1.3.3) correctly values the American contingent claim we must show that $Y_{\tau_t} = R^1_{0,\tau_t} Z_{\tau_t}$ is attainable by an admissible consumption-portfolio strategy (C, π) whose value is (1.3.3).

The Snell envelope Z is a process of class $D[0, T]$ and is regular ([**33**], Chapter 1, Definitions 4.8 and 4.12). Hence the Doob-Meyer decomposition holds,

$$Z_t = Z_0 + M_t - A_t, \ t \in [0, T],$$

where M is a Q-martingale and A is a continuous, nondecreasing process with $M_0 = A_0 = 0$. The Martingale Representation Theorem also implies that

$$M_t = \int_0^t \phi_s d\tilde{z}_s, \ t \in [0, T]$$

where $\phi \equiv \{\phi_t, \mathcal{F}_t : t \in [0, T]\}$ is a one-dimensional, $\mathcal{F}_t$-progressively measurable process. Selecting the portfolio and consumption (withdrawal) processes

$$\pi_{1t} \equiv R_{0,t}^{-1} \sigma_t^{-1} \phi_t$$

$$C_t \equiv \int_0^t R_{0,s}^{-1} dA_s,$$

defining the process

$$X_t \equiv R_{0,t}^{-1} Z_t,$$

and applying Itô's lemma to X yields, for $t \in [0, T]$,

$$\begin{aligned} dX_t &= r_t R_{0,t}^{-1} Z_t dt + R_{0,t}^{-1}(dM_t - dA_t) \\ &= r_t X_t dt + R_{0,t}^{-1}(\phi_t d\tilde{z}_t - dA_t) \\ &= r_t X_t dt + \pi_{1t} \sigma_t d\tilde{z}_t - dC_t. \end{aligned}$$

Hence X is a well-defined wealth process which corresponds to the admissible strategy (C, π). That is (C, π) is an admissible strategy which attains Y_{τ_t} and X is the corresponding wealth process. We conclude that

$$\begin{aligned} X_t \equiv R_{0,t}^{-1} Z_t &= R_{0,t}^{-1} \sup_{\tau \in \mathcal{S}_{t,T}} E^*[D_\tau | \mathcal{F}_t] \\ &= R_{0,t}^{-1} \sup_{\tau \in \mathcal{S}_{t,T}} E^*[R_{0,\tau} Y_\tau | \mathcal{F}_t] \\ &= \sup_{\tau \in \mathcal{S}_{t,T}} E^*[R_{t,\tau} Y_\tau | \mathcal{F}_t], \end{aligned}$$

for all $t \in [0, T]$. This establishes the valuation formula (1.3.3) of the theorem.

Remark 1.3.3 Theorem 1.3.2 and its proof also demonstrate that the discounted price of an American contingent claim without a flow of payments (i.e., with $f = 0$) is a Q-martingale prior to the optimal exercise time τ_0. It follows that $Z_t - Z_0 = \int_0^t (dM_t - dA_t)$, is a martingale prior to the exercise time τ_0. We conclude that $\int_0^t \mathbf{1}_{\{s < \tau_0\}} dA_s = 0$.

Theorem 1.3.2 states that the price of an American contingent claim is the present value of the payoffs received at or prior to the optimal exercise time. This representation of the price, although intuitive, is often impractical since the optimal stopping time, in most cases, cannot be computed explicitly. An alternative representation which emphasizes the gains from early exercise (prior to the maturity date T) often provides additional insights into the contributors to the value of such a claim.

The *early exercise premium representation* is, in fact, the Riesz decomposition of the Snell envelope. This decomposition was initially demonstrated by [22] for a class of stopping time problems. Myneni in [38] adapts their results to the valuation of American put options in an economy in which the interest rate is constant and the underlying asset price follows a geometric Brownian motion process. A generalization of the Riesz decomposition to a class of semimartingales adapted to a filtration satisfying the "usual conditions" appears in [**41**]. The results reported below are special cases of Rutkowski since the underlying uncertainty-information structure, in our economy, is given by the Brownian filtration introduced in Section 1.2.2.

Consider a contingent claim whose payoff Y, under the Q-measure, satisfies

$$Y_t = Y_0 + A_t(Y) + M_t(Y), \ t \in [0, T] \tag{1.3.5}$$

where $M(Y)$ is a Q-martingale and $A(Y)$ is a nondecreasing process null at 0; both $M(Y)$ and $A(Y)$ are progressively measurable processes of the Brownian filtration. For the example of a call option the exercise payoff is $Y = (S-K)^+$. This payoff can be decomposed in the form (1.3.5) by an application of the Tanaka-Meyer formula ([**33**], Chapter 3, Proposition 6.8).

Theorem 1.3.4 *Let $(0, Y) \in IS$. The value of the American contingent claim whose only payoff is the terminal payoff Y at the exercise time has the early exercise premium representation*

$$V_t(Y) = E^*[R_{t,T} Y_T | \mathcal{F}_t] + E^* \left[\int_{\tau_t}^T R_{t,s} \mathbf{1}_{\{\tau_s = s\}} (r_s Y_s ds - dA_s(Y)) | \mathcal{F}_t \right], \ t \in [0, T],$$
$$\tag{1.3.6}$$

where $\tau_t = \inf\{v \in [t, T] : D_v = Z_v\}$.

Equation (1.3.6) provides an intuitive decomposition of the price of the American contingent claim. It indicates that the price of the contract is the value of a European contingent claim with matching characteristics augmented by the gains from early exercise (the early exercise premium). As we shall see in the next section in a more specific context, the early exercise premium has a nice interpretation in the case of an American option.

Proof of Theorem 1.3.4 The proof follows from Lemma 1.3.5 below and from the fact that the process

$$Z_t + \int_0^t \mathbf{1}_{\{\tau_v = v\}} R_{0,v} [r_v Y_v dv - dA_v(Y)], \ t \in [0, T] \tag{1.3.7}$$

is a Q-martingale (see [**41**], Lemmas A.2, A.3, and A.4).

Lemma 1.3.5 *Let $Z_t \equiv \sup_{\tau \in \mathcal{S}_{t,T}} E^*[D_\tau | \mathcal{F}_t], \ t \in [0, T]$ and suppose that the process given in (1.3.7) is a Q-martingale. Then the representation (1.3.6) holds.*

Proof of Lemma 1.3.5 Since the process in (1.3.7) is a Q-martingale we can write

$$E^* \left[Z_T + \int_0^T \mathbf{1}_{\{\tau_v = v\}} R_{0,v} (r_v Y_v dv - dA_v(Y)) \right] = E^*[Z_0]. \tag{1.3.8}$$

By definition

$$Z_T = \sup_{\tau \in \mathcal{S}_{T,T}} E^*[D_\tau | \mathcal{F}_T] = E^*[D_T | \mathcal{F}_T] = D_T. \tag{1.3.9}$$

and

$$Z_0 = \sup_{\tau \in \mathcal{S}_{0,T}} E^*[D_\tau | \mathcal{F}_0] = E^*[D_{\tau_0} | \mathcal{F}_0]. \tag{1.3.10}$$

Substituting (1.3.9) and (1.3.10) in (1.3.8) yields

$$E^*[D_T] + E^* \left[\int_0^T \mathbf{1}_{\{\tau_v=v\}} R_{0,v}(r_v Y_v dv - dA_v(Y)) \right] = E^*[D_{\tau_0}]. \qquad (1.3.11)$$

By Theorem 1.3.2 the right-hand side of (1.3.11) equals $V_0(Y)$. Since $\mathbf{1}_{\{\tau_v=v\}} = 0$ in the random interval $[0, \tau_0]$ we conclude that the assertion of the lemma holds.

Corollary 1.3.6 *Contingent claims such that* $r_v Y_v dv - dA_v(Y) \le 0$ *for all* $v \in [0, T]$ *will never be exercised prior to the maturity date.*

Proof of Corollary 1.3.6 Under the condition stated early exercise can only lead to a reduction in the value of the contract. Hence, it is never optimal to exercise prior to maturity.

It is well known that it is suboptimal to exercise an American call option on a nondividend-paying stock prior to maturity [**37**]. For this contract $Y = (S - K)^+$ and, in the exercise region, $r_v Y_v dv - dA_v(Y) = r_v(S_v - K)dv - S_v r_v dv = -r_v K dv < 0$. Corollary 1.3.6 then applies and shows that early exercise is a suboptimal strategy.

An alternative to the early exercise premium representation of the American contingent claim is a decomposition which emphasizes the gains from delayed exercise. The *delayed exercise premium representation* for the American put option on a nondividend-paying asset and in a financial market with constant coefficients (constant interest rate and GBMP for the stock price) is due to [**14**]. The next theorem extends their results to the more general class of American contingent claims discussed in this section.

Theorem 1.3.7 *The value of the American contingent claim with payoff Y at the exercise time, such that $(0, Y) \in IS$, has the delayed exercise premium representation*

$$V_t(Y) = Y_t + E^* \left[\int_t^T R_{t,s} \mathbf{1}_{\{\tau_t > s\}} (dA_s(Y) - r_s Y_s ds) | \mathcal{F}_t \right], \quad t \in [0, T], \qquad (1.3.12)$$

where $\tau_t = \inf\{v \in [t, T] : S_v = Z_v\}$.

Proof of Theorem 1.3.7 The value of the contingent claim can always be written as
$$V_t(Y) = Y_t + E^*[(R_{t,\tau_t} Y_{\tau_t} - Y_t) | \mathcal{F}_t], \ t \in [0, T].$$
An application of Itô's lemma yields

$$V_t(Y) = Y_t + E^* \left[\int_t^{\tau_t} R_{t,s}(dA_s(Y) + dM_s(Y) - r_s Y_s ds) | \mathcal{F}_t \right], \ t \in [0, T].$$

The representation (1.3.12) follows since $M(Y)$ is a Q-martingale.

1.4 Standard American options: The GBMP model

We now focus on standard American option contracts in an economy in which the underlying asset price follows a geometric Brownian motion process (GBMP).

Consider an American call option with exercise price $K > 0$ and maturity date T, written on an underlying asset whose price S satisfies the stochastic differential equation (under the Q-measure)

$$dS_t = S_t[(r - \delta)dt + \sigma d\tilde{z}_t], \; t \in [0, T]; \; S_0 \text{ given.} \tag{1.4.1}$$

Here r, δ, and σ are constant parameters; r is the interest rate and δ represents the dividend rate paid on the asset. Since exercise can only be optimal when $S > K$ the option payoff upon exercise is $Y = (S - K)^+$.

Our first result characterizes the structure of the exercise region and its boundary. Since the environment is Markovian the state space is completely described by (S, t). Let $\mathcal{E} \equiv \{(S, t) \in \mathbf{R}^+ \times [0, T] : C(S, t) = (S - K)^+\}$ denote the immediate exercise region. Its complement is the continuation region $\mathcal{C} \equiv \{(S, t) \in \mathbf{R}^+ \times [0, T] : C(S, t) > (S - K)^+\}$.

Proposition 1.4.1 *The immediate exercise region has the following properties*

1. *right-connectedness: $(S, t) \in \mathcal{E}$ implies $(S, s) \in \mathcal{E}$ for all $t \in [0, T]$ and $s \in [t, T]$.*

2. *up-connectedness: $(S, t) \in \mathcal{E}$ implies $(\lambda S, t) \in \mathcal{E}$ for $\lambda \geq 1$, for all $t \in [0, T]$.*

3. *Suppose that $S \leq \max\{K, (r/\delta)K\}$. Then $(S, t) \notin \mathcal{E}$, for all $t \in [0, T]$.*

Proof of Proposition 1.4.1 Recall that $\mathcal{S}_{s,T}$ denotes the set of stopping times of the Brownian filtration with values in $[s, T]$.

1. Since $s \geq t$ we have $\mathcal{S}_{s,T} \subseteq \mathcal{S}_{t,T}$ and therefore $C(S, t) \geq C(S, s)$. By assumption, immediate exercise is optimal at t. Thus $(S - K)^+ \geq C(S, s)$.

2. Consider $S^1 > S^2$ and suppose that $(S^2, t) \in \mathcal{E}$ while $(S^1, t) \notin \mathcal{E}$. Let τ_1 denote the optimal stopping time at (S^1, t). For $s \geq t$ define the exponential process $N_{t,s} \equiv \exp[(r - \delta - \frac{1}{2}\sigma^2)(s - t) + \sigma(\tilde{z}_s - \tilde{z}_t)]$ and note that $S_s = S_t N_{t,s}$. We have the following sequence of relations

$$
\begin{aligned}
C(S^1, t) &= E^*[e^{-r(\tau_1 - t)}(S^1 N_{t,\tau_1} - K)^+] \quad \text{(optimality of } \tau_1 \text{ at } (S^1, t)) \\
&= E^*[e^{-r(\tau_1 - t)}(S^2 N_{t,\tau_1} + (S^1 - S^2)N_{t,\tau_1} - K)^+] \\
&\leq E^*[e^{-r(\tau_1 - t)}(S^2 N_{t,\tau_1} - K)^+] + E^*[e^{-r(\tau_1 - t)}(S^1 - S^2)N_{t,\tau_1}] \\
&\qquad \text{(since } (a + b)^+ \leq a^+ + b^+) \\
&\leq C(S^2, t) + (S^1 - S^2)E^*[e^{-r(\tau_1 - t)}N_{t,\tau_1}] \\
&\qquad \text{(suboptimality of } \tau_1 \text{ at } (S^2, t)) \\
&\leq C(S^2, t) + S^1 - S^2 \\
&\qquad (S^1 - S^2 > 0 \text{ and supermartingale property of } S) \\
&\leq (S^2 - K) + S^1 - S^2 = S^1 - K \\
&\qquad \text{(optimality of immediate exercise at } (S^2, t))
\end{aligned}
$$

Hence $C(S^1, t) \leq S^1 - K$, which contradicts the assumed suboptimality of immediate exercise at (S^1, t).

3. Suppose that $0 < S \leq K$. Since $P[S_v > K] > 0$ for some $v \in [t, T]$ immediate exercise is a suboptimal policy. Suppose that $K < S \leq (r/\delta)K$ and assume that immediate exercise is optimal, i.e., $C(S, t) = S - K$. Consider the portfolio consisting of 1 call option, 1 share of the stock held

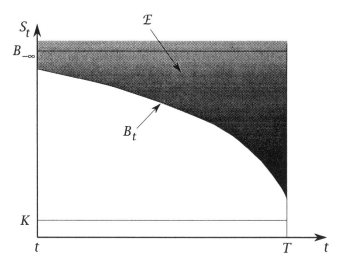

Figure 1.4.2 Exercise Region for a Standard American Option

short and K dollars invested at the riskfree rate. Define the stopping time $\tau \equiv \tau_{(r/\delta)K} = \inf\{v \in [t,T] : S_v = (r/\delta)K\}$ or $\tau_{(r/\delta)K} = T$ if no such time exists. Suppose that we liquidate this portfolio at the stopping time τ. The cash flows generated by this investment strategy are

	Time t	Time τ
Buy call	$-C(S,t) = -(S-K)$	$(S_\tau - K)^+$
Sell stock	$+S$	$-S_\tau - \int_t^\tau e^{r(\tau-v)}\delta S_v dv$
Invest K	$-K$	$K + \int_t^\tau e^{r(\tau-v)}rK dv$
Total	0	$(K - S_\tau)^+ + \int_t^\tau e^{r(\tau-v)}(rK - \delta S_v)dv$

Since $(rK - \delta S_v) > 0$ for all $v < \tau$ this strategy is an arbitrage strategy. Since the existence of an equilibrium implies the absence of arbitrage opportunities it must be the case that $C(S,t) > (S-K)$, i.e., immediate exercise is a suboptimal strategy.

An illustration of the exercise region and corresponding boundary for a standard American option is given in Figure 1.4.2. The next proposition states some basic properties of the price function. Properties of the call and put price functions in more general market models are explored in detail in [**26**].

Proposition 1.4.3 *Let C(S,t) denote the value of the American call option. We have*

1. *$C(S,t)$ is continuous on $\mathbf{R}^+ \times [0,T]$.*

2. *$C(\cdot,t)$ is nondecreasing and convex on $\mathbf{R}^+$ for all $t \in [0,T]$.*

3. *$C(S,\cdot)$ is nonincreasing on $[0,T]$ for all $S \in \mathbf{R}^+$.*

4. *$0 \le \partial C(S,t)/\partial S \le 1$ on $\mathbf{R}^+ \times [0,T]$; $\partial C(S,t)/\partial S = 1$ for (S,t) in the interior of $\mathcal{E}$.*

5. $\partial C(S, t)/\partial S$ is continuous on $\mathbf{R}^+$ for all $t \in [0, T)$.

Proof of Proposition 1.4.3

1. This follows from the continuity of the option payoff function and the continuity of the flow of the stochastic differential equation (1.4.1) relative to the initial values.

2. This follows from the monotonicity (increasing) of the flow and the increasing and convex structure of the payoff.

3. This is a straightforward counterpart of Proposition 1.4.1 (1).

4. Consider (S^1, t) and (S^2, t) such that $S^1 > S^2$. For any stopping time $\tau \in \mathcal{S}_{0,T}$ we have

$$0 \le [(S_\tau^1 - K)^+ - (S_\tau^2 - K)^+] \le (S_\tau^1 - S_\tau^2) = (S^1 - S^2)N_{t,\tau}.$$

In particular this holds for the optimal stopping time τ_1 associated with (S^1, t). Hence, we can write

$$\begin{aligned}
0 &\le C(S^1, t) - C(S^2, t) \\
&= E^*[e^{-r(\tau_1 - t)}(S^1 N_{t,\tau_1} - K)^+ | \mathcal{F}_t] \\
&\quad - E^*[e^{-r(\tau_2 - t)}(S^2 N_{t,\tau_2} - K)^+ | \mathcal{F}_t] \\
&\le E^*[e^{-r(\tau_1 - t)}(S^1 - S^2)N_{t,\tau_1} | \mathcal{F}_t] \\
&\qquad \text{(suboptimality of } \tau_1 \text{ at } (S^2, t)) \\
&= (S^1 - S^2)E^*[e^{-r(\tau_1 - t)} N_{t,\tau_1} | \mathcal{F}_t] \\
&\le (S^1 - S^2),
\end{aligned}$$

where the last inequality follows since $S^1 - S^2 > 0$ and since the discounted price of a dividend-paying asset is a Q-supermartingale. Dividing both sides by $S^1 - S^2$ proves the statement (this argument also establishes the continuity of the option price with respect to S).

Property (1) implies that the immediate exercise region is a closed set (the continuation region is an open set). We conclude that the boundary of the immediate exercise region is well defined as $B \equiv \{B_t : t \in [0, T]\}$ where $B_t \equiv \inf\{S : (S, t) \in \mathcal{E}\}$ and belongs to $\mathcal{E}$. The boundary has the following structure.

Proposition 1.4.4 *The boundary of the immediate exercise region is continuous, nonincreasing and has limiting values* $\lim_{t \uparrow T} B_t = \max\{K, (r/\delta)K\}$ *and* $\lim_{T-t \uparrow \infty} B_t = B_{-\infty} \equiv K(b + f)/(b + f - \sigma^2)$ *where* $b \equiv \delta - r + \frac{1}{2}\sigma^2$ *and* $f \equiv (b^2 + 2r\sigma^2)^{\frac{1}{2}}$.

The continuity and monotonocity of the boundary B follow from Proposition 1.4.1 properties (1) and (2). The limiting values are obtained from the recursive equation (1.4.5) for the exercise boundary in Theorem 1.4.5 below. Note that the optimal exercise boundary for the deterministic problem with $\sigma = 0$ is $\max\{K, (r/\delta)K\}$. For the stochastic problem the remaining uncertainty faced by the investor $\sigma(T - t)$ converges to zero as $t \uparrow T$ and we expect the optimal exercise boundary to converge to the boundary for the deterministic problem. This is the intuition underlying this limiting result stated in Proposition 1.4.4. The American option exercise boundary is studied in detail in [1] and [4]. See also [44].

In the GMBP case Theorem 1.3.4 specializes as follows.

Theorem 1.4.5 ([**35**], [**30**], [**14**]) *Suppose that the underlying asset price follows the geometric Brownian motion process (1.4.1) and that the interest rate is constant. The value of an American call option has the early exercise premium representation*

$$C(S_t, t) = C^e(S_t, t)$$
$$+ \int_t^T (\delta S_t e^{-\delta(s-t)} N(d_2(S_t, B_s, s-t)) - rKe^{-r(s-t)} N(d_3(S_t, B_s, s-t)))ds,$$
$$(1.4.2)$$

for $t \in [0, T]$, where $C^e(S, t)$ represents the Black-Scholes value of a European call option (Equation (1.2.19)) and

$$d_2(S_t, B_s, s-t) = (\log(S_t/B_s) + (r - \delta + \frac{1}{2}\sigma^2)(s-t))/(\sigma\sqrt{s-t}) \qquad (1.4.3)$$

$$d_3(S_t, B_s, s-t) = d_2(S_t, B_s, s-t) - \sigma\sqrt{s-t}. \qquad (1.4.4)$$

The immediate exercise boundary B solves the backward nonlinear integral equation

$$B_t - K = C^e(B_t, t)$$
$$+ \int_t^T (\delta B_t e^{-\delta(s-t)} N(d_2(B_t, B_s, s-t)) - rKe^{-r(s-t)} N(d_3(B_t, B_s, s-t)))ds,$$
$$(1.4.5)$$

subject to the boundary condition $B_T = \max\{K, (r/\delta)K\}$.

Proof of Theorem 1.4.5 Proposition 1.4.1 implies $B \geq \max\{K, (r/\delta)K\}$. Hence $Y = (S - K)^+$ equals $S - K$ in the exercise region. If follows that $dY_t = S_t[(r-\delta)dt + \sigma d\tilde{z}_t]$ in the exercise region, i.e., $dA_t(Y) = S_t(r-\delta)dt$ on $\{S_t \geq B_t\}$. Theorem 1.3.4 then implies

$$C(S_t, t) = C^e(S_t, t) + E^* \left[\int_t^T e^{-r(v-t)} [r(S_v - K) - (r - \delta)S_v] \mathbf{1}_{\{S_v \geq B_v\}} dv | \mathcal{F}_t \right]$$

$$= C^e(S_t, t) + E^* \left[\int_t^T e^{-r(v-t)} [\delta S_v - rK] \mathbf{1}_{\{S_v \geq B_v\}} dv | \mathcal{F}_t \right],$$
$$(1.4.6)$$

Under the GBMP assumption the expectation in (1.4.6) can be computed explicitly. This leads to (1.4.2). The recursive equation for the optimal exercise boundary follows from the boundary condition $C(B, t) = B - K$.

When the option maturity becomes infinite the option price expression (1.4.2) simplifies as follows ([**42**] and [**37**]).

Corollary 1.4.6 (American options with infinite maturity) *Consider an American call option with infinite maturity. Its value is $C(S, t) = (B_\infty - K)(S/B_\infty)^{2\alpha/\sigma^2}$, where $B_\infty = K(b+f)/(b+f-\sigma^2)$, $\alpha = \frac{1}{2}(b+f)$, $b = \delta - r + \frac{1}{2}\sigma^2$, and $f = \sqrt{b^2 + 2r\sigma^2}$.*

Proof of Corollary 1.4.6 When $T \uparrow \infty$ the immediate exercise boundary becomes time independent: $B = B_\infty$. Then $d_2(B_\infty, B_\infty, s-t) = (r - \delta + \frac{1}{2}\sigma^2)(s-t)/(\sigma\sqrt{s-t})$ and $d_3(B_\infty, B_\infty, s-t) = d_2(B_\infty, B_\infty, s-t) - \sigma\sqrt{s-t}$ are independent of B_∞. Since the European call option value also converges to 0 the recursive equation (1.4.5) becomes linear in B_∞ and has solution $B_\infty = K(b+f)/(b+f-\sigma^2)$.

The value of the option then follows from (1.4.2): the early exercise premium simplifies to $(B_\infty - K)(S/B_\infty)^{2\alpha/\sigma^2}$.

The next proposition gives a relationship between American puts and calls which enables us to infer the value of a put on a dividend-paying asset by a simple reparametrization of the American call pricing function. This symmetry result is a variation of the international put-call equivalence [25] and was originally proved in [35].

Proposition 1.4.7 (American put-call symmetry) *Consider American put and call options written on the same underlying asset whose price satisfies (1.4.1). Suppose that these options have the same maturity and the same exercise price. Let $P(S, K, r, \delta, T)$ and $C(S, K, r, \delta, T)$ denote the respective price functions. Then*

$$P(S, K, r, \delta, T) = C(K, S, \delta, r, T).$$

Corollary 1.4.7 implies that a put with exercise price K and maturity T, written on a stock with dividend rate δ and price S in a market with interest rate r has the same value as a call with exercise price S and maturity T written on a stock with dividend rate r and price K when the interest rate is δ.

The model for the underlying asset price in (1.4.1) allows for dividends which are paid at a continuous rate. This type of model has been used to value foreign currency options, futures options, and index options. See, e.g., [29] for a description of these contracts. Analytical solutions for American options in the case of discrete dividends are given in [39], [24] and [45]. Numerical techniques for the valuation of American options were initiated in [43] and [8, 9]. Convergence of the Brennan and Schwartz method is proved in [31]. Probably the most widely used numerical technique is the binomial method developed in [17] and [18]. Convergence of the binomial method for pricing American options is proved in [2]. A new numerical technique and a comparison of existing methods is given in [11].

Pricing results for American bond and yield options are given in [15]. Results for American options on multiple assets are derived in [12]. The pricing of American capped options is considered in the next section.

1.5 American capped options

In the past few years several contracts with cap provisions have been issued by financial institutions. One example is the MILES contract (Mexican Index-Linked Euro Security). This contract is an American call option on the dollar value of the Mexican stock index. The contract is somewhat unusual since it has both a cap and a restriction on the exercise period.

Other examples of capped options are the capped options on the S&P 100 and S&P 500 indices that were introduced by the Chicago Board of Options Exchange (CBOE) in November 1991. These capped index options combine a European exercise feature (the holder of the security cannot exercise until the maturity of the contract) with an automatic exercise provision. The automatic exercise provision is triggered if the index value exceeds the cap at the close of the day. See [23] for a critical analysis of these options. Additional examples of European capped options include the range forward contract, collar loans, barrier options, indexed notes and index currency option notes (see [7] and [40]).

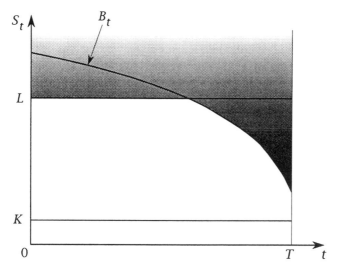

Figure 1.5.2 Exercise Region for an American Capped Call Option

Our treatment in this section follows [10]. We first consider options with constant caps (subsection 1.5.1), then extend the analysis to caps that grow at a constant rate (subsection 1.5.2), and conclude with capped options on nondividend-paying assets with stochastic volatility (subsection 1.5.3). In subsections 1.5.1 and 1.5.2, we suppose that the economy under consideration is the economy of Section 1.4 in which the interest rate is constant and the underlying asset price follows the geometric Brownian motion process (1.4.1).

1.5.1 Capped options with a constant cap

We consider an American capped call option with maturity date T, exercise price K and constant cap L with $L > K$. Upon exercise this contract pays $(S \wedge L - K)^+$. Let B^L and $C^L(S,t)$ denote the optimal exercise boundary and the price of the capped option, respectively. The optimal exercise boundary is characterized in Theorem 1.5.1 and illustrated in Figure 1.5.2.

Theorem 1.5.1 *Consider an American capped call option with maturity date T, exercise price K and constant cap equal to L with $L > K$. The optimal exercise boundary B^L is given by*

$$B^L = L \wedge B, \tag{1.5.1}$$

where B denotes the optimal exercise boundary of an American uncapped call option with same maturity date and exercise price.

Proof of Theorem 1.5.1 Case (i): Suppose first that $S \geq L$. Then immediate exercise is optimal since the exercise payoff is $(S \wedge L - K)^+ = L - K$, which is the maximum payoff attainable.

Case (ii): Suppose that $B \leq S < L$. Since $(S \wedge L - K)^+ \leq (S - K)^+$ the inequality

$$C^L(S,t) \leq C(S,t) \tag{1.5.2}$$

always holds. In the region under consideration immediate exercise is optimal for the holder of the uncapped option. Thus $C^L(S,t) \leq (S - K)^+ = (S - K)$. Since immediate exercise is a feasible strategy for the holder of the uncapped option with a payoff equal to $(S \wedge L - K)^+ = (S - K)^+ = (S - K)$, we conclude that immediate exercise is optimal for the uncapped option as well (if not there exists a waiting strategy which dominates immediate exercise for the capped option, hence for the uncapped option — a contradiction since we are in the case $S \geq B$).

Case (iii): Suppose that $S < B \wedge L$. We must show that immediate exercise is suboptimal. Consider first the case $L > \max\{(r/\delta)K, K\}$. Let $B(T, t)$ denote the exercise boundary for an uncapped option with exercise price K and maturity date T. Recall that $B(T, t)$ is a strictly decreasing function of time and converges to $K \vee (r/\delta)K$ as t converges to T. Hence, in the case under consideration, we can always find a shorter maturity T_0, $T_0 \leq T$, such that $S_t < B(T_0, t) < L$. Clearly the strategy of exercising at the first hitting time of the set $[B(T_0, t), \infty)$ is feasible for the holder of the capped option. This strategy also has the same payoff as the uncapped option with shorter maturity T_0. We conclude that

$$C(S, t, T_0) \leq C^L(S, t). \tag{1.5.3}$$

Since immediate exercise is suboptimal for the shorter maturity uncapped option when $S < B(T_0, t)$ we must have $(S - K)^+ < C^L(S, t)$. That is, immediate exercise is suboptimal for the capped option. Consider next the case $L \leq (r/\delta)K$. Let τ denote the minimum of T and of the first hitting time of the set $[L, \infty)$. The policy of exercising at τ dominates immediate exercise since $\delta S_v - rK < 0$ for $v \in [t, \tau)$.

Since the early exercise strategy is fully identified, the valuation of the contract is easy to perform. Let t^* denote the solution to the equation

$$B(T, t) = L, \tag{1.5.4}$$

if an interior solution in $[0, T]$ exists. If $B(T, t) < L$ for all $t \in [0, T]$ set $t^* = 0$. If $B(T, t) > L$ for all $t \in [0, T]$ set $t^* = T$.

The next theorem provides a valuation formula for the American capped call option.

Theorem 1.5.3 *Consider an American capped call option with maturity date T, exercise price K and constant cap equal to L $(L > K)$. For $S \geq L \wedge B$ the option value is $(S \wedge L) - K$. For $S < L \wedge B$ and $t \geq t^*$ the option value is $C^L(S, t) = C(S, t)$. For $S < L \wedge B$ and $t < t^*$ the option is worth $C^L(S, t)$ given by*

$$(L - K)E^*[e^{-r(\tau_L - t)}\mathbf{1}_{\{\tau_L < t^*\}}|\mathcal{F}_t] + E^*[e^{-r(t^* - t)}C(S_{t^*}, t^*)\mathbf{1}_{\{\tau_L \geq t^*\}}|\mathcal{F}_t], \tag{1.5.5}$$

where $\tau_L \equiv \inf\{v \in [t, T] : S_v = L\}$ denotes the first hitting time of L in $[t, T]$ and $\tau_L \equiv T$ if no such time exists in $[t, T]$. The representation formula in (1.5.5) can be simplified by computing the expectations explicitly

$$C^L(S, t) = (L - K)(\lambda^{2\phi/\sigma^2}N(d_0) + \lambda^{2\alpha/\sigma^2}N(d_0 + 2f\sqrt{t^* - t}/\sigma^2))$$
$$+ e^{-r(t^* - t)}\int_0^L C(x, t^*)u(x, t, t^*)dx \tag{1.5.6}$$

where

$$u(x, t, t^*) = \left(n(d_1^-(x)) - \lambda^{1-2(r-\delta)/\sigma^2}n(d_1^+(x))\right)/(x\sigma\sqrt{t^* - t}) \tag{1.5.7}$$

$$d_0 = \left(\log(\lambda) - f(t^* - t)\right)/(\sigma\sqrt{t^* - t}) \tag{1.5.8}$$

$$d_1^\pm(x) = \left(\pm\log(\lambda) - \log(L) + \log(x) + b(t^* - t)\right)/(\sigma\sqrt{t^* - t}), \tag{1.5.9}$$

and $b = \delta - r + \frac{1}{2}\sigma^2$, $f = \sqrt{b^2 + 2r\sigma^2}$, $\phi = \frac{1}{2}(b - f)$, $\alpha = \frac{1}{2}(b + f)$, and $\lambda = S/L$.

An alternative decomposition which draws on Theorems 1.3.4 and 1.4.5 relates the value of the American capped option to the value of a capped option with automatic exercise at the cap.

Theorem 1.5.4 (Early exercise premium representation) *Let $C^{ae}(S, t, L)$ denote the value of a capped option with automatic exercise at the cap (see formula (1.5.11) below). For $S < L \wedge B$ and $t \in [0, T]$, the value of the American capped option is given by*

$$C^L(S, t) = C^{ae}(S, t, L) + E^*\left[\int_t^{\tau_L} e^{-r(v-t)}(\delta S_v - rK)\mathbf{1}_{\{L \geq S_v \geq B_v\}} dv \Big| \mathcal{F}_t\right], \quad (1.5.10)$$

where $\tau_L \equiv \inf\{v \in [t, T] : S_v = L\}$ denotes the first hitting time of L in $[t, T]$, and $\tau_L \equiv T$ if no such time exists in $[t, T]$.

This decomposition of the American option value is similar to the early exercise premium representation for standard American options (Theorem 1.4.5). It differs in that it relates the value of the option contract to the value of a contract which may be automatically exercised before the maturity date (the standard representation uses the value of a European option with exercise at the maturity date as the benchmark).

The next result shows that the valuation formulas (1.5.6) and (1.5.10) simplify in the case of sufficiently low dividends.

Corollary 1.5.5 (American capped call valuation with low dividends) *Suppose that $\delta \leq rK/L$. For $S < L$ and $t \in [0, T]$, the value of the American capped call option equals the value of the corresponding capped call option with automatic exercise at the cap*

$$
\begin{aligned}
C^L(S, t) &= C^{ae}(S, t, L) \\
&= (L - K)(\lambda^{2\phi/\sigma^2} N(d_0) + \lambda^{2\alpha/\sigma^2} N(d_0 + 2f\sqrt{\tau}/\sigma)) \\
&\quad + Se^{-\delta\tau}(N(d_1^-(L) - \sigma\sqrt{\tau}) - N(d_1^-(K) - \sigma\sqrt{\tau})) \\
&\quad - \lambda^{-2(r-\delta)/\sigma^2} Le^{-\delta\tau}(N(d_1^+(L) - \sigma\sqrt{\tau}) - N(d_1^+(K) - \sigma\sqrt{\tau})) \\
&\quad - Ke^{-r\tau}(N(d_1^-(L)) - N(d_1^-(K)) - \lambda^{1-2(r-\delta)/\sigma^2}(N(d_1^+(L)) - N(d_1^+(K)))).
\end{aligned}
$$
$$(1.5.11)$$

In (1.5.11) the expressions for d_0 and $d_1^{\pm}(x)$ are the same as in (1.5.8)–(1.5.9) but with $\tau = T - t$ replacing $t^* - t$. The expressions for b, f, ϕ, and α are the same as in Theorem 1.5.4.

Remark 1.5.6 The value of a European capped call option with strike price K, cap L, and maturity T (the option with payoff $(S_T \wedge L - K)^+$ at date T) is given by

$$
\begin{aligned}
C^e(S, t, L) &= Se^{-\delta(T-t)}(N(d_1^-(L) - \sigma\sqrt{T-t}) - N(d_1^-(K) - \sigma\sqrt{T-t})) \\
&\quad - Ke^{-r(T-t)}(1 - N(d_1^-(K))) + Le^{-r(T-t)}(1 - N(d_1^-(L))).
\end{aligned}
$$
$$(1.5.12)$$

The European capped option value can serve as a benchmark to measure the gains from early exercise (prior to maturity) embedded in the American capped option value. The early exercise premium is particularly simple to compute in the case of low dividends (formula (1.5.11)).

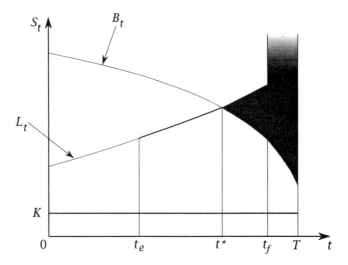

Figure 1.5.10 Exercise Region for a (t_e, t^*, t_f) Policy

Remark 1.5.7 If $L \uparrow \infty$ the European capped call option value $C^e(S, t, L)$ converges to the Black-Scholes formula adjusted for dividends (equation (1.2.20)).

1.5.2 Capped options with growing caps

We now consider the class of American capped options whose caps grow at a constant rate. Suppose that

$$L_t = L_0 e^{gt}, \ t \in [0, T], \tag{1.5.14}$$

where we assume that $L_0 > K$. Let t^* denote the solution to the equation

$$B(T, t) = L_t, \tag{1.5.15}$$

if an interior solution in $[0, T]$ exists. If $B(T, t) < L_t$ for all $t \in [0, T]$ set $t^* = 0$. If $B(T, t) > L_t$ for all $t \in [0, T]$ set $t^* = T$.

In order to determine the optimal exercise region we need to consider the class of exercise strategies defined next and illustrated in Figure 1.5.10.

Definition 1.5.8 $((t_e, t^*, t_f)$ Exercise Policy) Let t_e and t_f satisfy $0 \le t_e \le t_f \le T$ and $t_e \le t^* \le T$. Define the stopping time τ_1 by $\inf\{v \in [t_e, t_f] : S_v = L_v\}$ or if no such v exists set $\tau_1 = T$. Set the stopping time τ_2 equal to t_f if $S_{t_f} \ge L_{t_f}$ otherwise set $\tau_2 = T$. Define the stopping time τ_3 by $\inf\{v \in [t^*, T] : S_v = B_v\}$ or if no such v exists set $\tau_3 = T$. An exercise policy is a (t_e, t^*, t_f)-policy if the option is exercised at the stopping time $\tau_1 \wedge \tau_2 \wedge \tau_3$.

Theorem 1.5.9 Consider an American capped call option with exercise price K, maturity date T and cap given by equation (1.5.14). Then the optimal exercise strategy is a (t_e, t^*, t_f)-policy.

Proof of Theorem 1.5.9 Case (i): Suppose first that $B \le S < L$. Then the same argument as in the proof of Theorem 1.5.1, case (ii) applies and demonstrates that immediate exercise is an optimal strategy.

Case (ii): Consider now the case $S < B \wedge L$ and suppose that $(r/\delta)K > K$. If $L_t \geq (r/\delta)K$ the argument in the proof of Theorem 1.5.1, case (iii) applies. If $L_t < (r/\delta)K$ the policy of exercising at the stopping time τ equal to the first hitting time of the set $[(r/\delta)K \wedge L, \infty)$ or T if no such time exists, dominates immediate exercise since $\delta S_v - rK < 0$ for $v \in [t, \tau)$. In the case $(r/\delta)K \leq K$ we have $L_t > K$ for all $t \in [0, T]$ and the argument of Theorem 1.5.1, case (iii), applies again.

Case (iii): Suppose now that $S > L$. It can be verified that the discounted payoff function $e^{-rt}(L_t - K)$ is unimodal with a maximum at

$$t_f = \mathrm{argmax}_{t \in [0,T]} e^{-rt}(L_t - K)$$

and is strictly increasing for $t < t_f$ and strictly decreasing for $t \geq t_f$. Hence if $t \geq t_f$ immediate exercise strictly dominates any waiting strategy. If $t < t_f$ the strategy of exercising at the first hitting time of L or at t_f strictly dominates immediate exercise.

Case (iv): Finally, suppose that immediate exercise is optimal at some time $t < t^*$ when $S = L$. Then it is optimal to exercise at all $v \in [t, t^*]$ when $S_v = L_v$. Suppose not, i.e., suppose that there exists u such that $S_u = L_u$ and $C^L(S_u, u) > (L_u - K)$. At t we have

$$L_t - K = C^L(S_t, t)$$
$$\geq C^L(S_t, t, T - (u - t)) \quad \text{(shorter maturity option)}$$
$$= C^H(S_t, u, T) \quad \text{(H is L translated by } u - t)$$
$$\geq C^L(S_u, u) - (L_u - L_t). \quad \text{(see Lemma 1.5.11 below)}$$

If immediate exercise is suboptimal at u then $C^L(S_u, u) > L_u - K$ so that $(L_t - K) > (L_u - K) - (L_u - L_t) = L_t - K$, a contradiction.

Lemma 1.5.11 *Suppose that the underlying asset price S satisfies (1.4.1). Consider two American capped call options written on S, with common maturity date T and exercise price K, and respective caps L and H satisfying (1.5.14), $L_0 > H_0$. Let $S_0^1 = L_0$ and $S_0^2 = H_0$. Then $C^L(S_0^1, 0) \leq C^H(S_0^2, 0) + L_0 - H_0$.*

Proof of Lemma 1.5.11 For any stopping time $\tau \in \mathcal{S}_{0,T}$ we have $0 \leq ((S_\tau^1 \wedge L_\tau - K)^+ - (S_\tau^2 \wedge H_\tau - K)^+] \leq (S_\tau^1 \wedge L_\tau - S_\tau^2 \wedge H_\tau) = S_0^1 N_{0,\tau} \wedge L_0 e^{g\tau} - S_0^2 N_{0,\tau} \wedge H_0 e^{g\tau}$. Since $S_0^1 = L_0$ and $S_0^2 = H_0$ the right-hand side of the inequality equals $(S_0^1 - S_0^2)(N_{0,\tau} \wedge e^{g\tau})$, which is bounded above by $(S_0^1 - S_0^2)N_{0,\tau}$. This upper bound on the payoff holds, in particular, for the optimal stopping time τ_1 associated with $(S_0^1, 0)$. Hence, we can write

$$0 \leq C^L(S_0^1, 0) - C^H(S_0^2, 0)$$
$$= E^*[e^{-r\tau_1}(S_0^1 N_{0,\tau_1} \wedge L_0 e^{g\tau_1} - K)^+ | \mathcal{F}_0]$$
$$\quad - E^*[e^{-r(\tau_2 - t)}(S_0^2 N_{0,\tau_2} \wedge H_0 e^{g\tau_2} - K)^+ | \mathcal{F}_0]$$
$$\leq E^*[e^{-r\tau_1}(S_0^1 - S_0^2)N_{0,\tau_1} | \mathcal{F}_0] \quad \text{(suboptimality of } \tau_1 \text{ at } (S_0^2, 0))$$
$$\leq S_0^1 - S_0^2. \quad \text{(Q-supermartingale property of } R_{0,t} S_t)$$

By assumption $S_0^1 = L_0$ and $S_0^2 = H_0$. So Lemma 1.5.11 follows.

Theorem 1.5.9 shows that the optimal stopping time is a (t_e, t^*, t_f) exercise policy. The parameters t^* and t_f are completely determined from the structure of the capped option payoff, the cap process, the underlying asset process, and the interest rate. So $t_e \in [0, t^*]$ is the only parameter which remains to be determined. Thus, pricing an American capped call option has been reduced to the identification of t_e, which is a simple univariate optimization problem. The valuation formula for this contract is given in the next theorem.

Theorem 1.5.12 (Valuation of American capped option with growing cap) *Define*

$$t_f \equiv \mathrm{argmax}_{t \in [0,T]} \{e^{-rt}(L_t - K)\}. \tag{1.5.16}$$

The value of the American capped option with growing cap is given by

$$C^L(S, 0) = \max_{t_e} \{C^L(t_e, t^*, t_f) : t_e \in [0, t^* \wedge t_f]\} \tag{1.5.17}$$

where

$$C^L(t_e, t^*, t_f) = E^*[e^{-r(t_e-t)}\{C^u \mathbf{1}_{\{S_{t_e} > L_{t_e}\}} + C^d \mathbf{1}_{\{S_{t_e} \leq L_{t_e}\}}\}|\mathcal{F}_t]. \tag{1.5.18}$$

and C^u and C^d are the values at time t_e in the events $\{S_{t_e} > L_{t_e}\}$ and $\{S_{t_e} \leq L_{t_e}\}$, respectively.

Explicit formulas for C^u and C^d are given in [**10**].

1.5.3 Capped options on nondividend-paying assets with stochastic volatility

In this subsection we consider a fairly general class of American capped options written on nondividend-paying assets with stochastic volatility. The underlying asset price S satisfies (under the Q-measure)

$$dS_t = S_t(rdt + \sigma_t d\tilde{z}_t), t \in [0, T]; \ S_0 \text{ given.} \tag{1.5.17}$$

The volatility process $\sigma \equiv \{\sigma_t, \mathcal{F}_t : t \in [0, T]\}$ is a progressively measurable, bounded above and bounded away from zero (P-a.s.). The interest rate r is constant and nonnegative.

The capped call option under consideration has a payoff $(S \wedge L - K)^+$, where L satisfies

$$dL_t = L_t g_t dt, t \in [0, T], \ L_0 \text{ given.} \tag{1.5.18}$$

We assume that the growth rate of the cap, g, is a progressively measurable process such that $L_t > K$ for all $t \in [0, T]$ and which satisfies the condition

$$(g_t - r)L_t + rK < 0, t \in [0, T]. \tag{1.5.19}$$

The model (1.5.17)–(1.5.19) for the underlying asset price and for the cap is relatively general. It allows for a stochastic volatility of the underlying asset price as well as a stochastic growth rate of the cap. The factor underlying the stochastic behavior of the volatility and the cap is the same Brownian motion which affects the stock price. Hence, the model remains one of complete markets. The cap's growth rate may take positive as well as negative values as long as condition (1.5.19) is satisfied. This condition is a restriction on the growth rate of the cap which is clearly satisfied if the cap is constant or decreasing. It is satisfied even when the growth rate of the cap is positive as long as it is not too large.

For this model we have the following result.

Theorem 1.5.13 *Consider an American capped call option with stochastic cap given by (1.5.18)–(1.5.19) when the interest rate is constant and the underlying asset price satisfies (1.5.17). The optimal exercise boundary is $B^L = L$. If $S \geq L$ immediate exercise is optimal and $C^L(S,t) = L - K$. If $S < L$ the optimal exercise policy is described by the stopping time τ_L where $\tau_L \equiv \inf\{v \in [t,T] : S_v = L_v\}$, or $\tau_L \equiv T$ if no such time exists. For $S < L$ and for all $t \in [0,T]$, the value of the capped option is*

$$C^L(S,t) = E^*[e^{-r(\tau_L-t)}(L_{\tau_L} - K)\mathbf{1}_{\{\tau_L<T\}}|\mathcal{F}_t] + E^*[e^{-r(T-t)}(S_T-K)^+\mathbf{1}_{\{\tau_L\geq T\}}|\mathcal{F}_t]. \tag{1.5.20}$$

Proof of Theorem 1.5.13 We must show the optimality of stopping at the first hitting time of the cap. The valuation formula (1.5.20) is the value under that exercise policy.

(i) Suppose first that $S < L$ and assume that immediate exercise is optimal. Consider the investment strategy described below along with the exercise policy τ_L defined in the theorem

	Time t	Time $\tau_L < T$	Time $\tau_L \geq T$
Buy call	$-C(S,t)$	$L_{\tau_L} - K$	$(S_T - K)^+$
Sell stock	$+S$	S_{τ_L}	$-S_T$
Invest K	$-K$	$Ke^{r\tau_L}$	$Ke^{r(T-t)}$
Total	0	$K(e^{r\tau_L} - 1)$	$-S_T\mathbf{1}_{\{S_T<K\}}$ $+K(e^{r(T-t)} - \mathbf{1}_{\{S_T\geq K\}})$

Since the payoff on the event $\tau_L \geq T$ is bounded below by

$$-K\mathbf{1}_{\{S_T<K\}} + K(e^{r(T-t)} - \mathbf{1}_{\{S_T\geq K\}}) = K(e^{r(T-t)} - 1)$$

and since $r > 0$ the strategy outlined is an arbitrage strategy. The absence of arbitrage opportunities in equilibrium implies that immediate exercise is a suboptimal strategy.

(ii) Consider now the case $S \geq L$. By Itô's lemma the discounted payoff $\psi_t \equiv e^{-rt}(L_t - K)$ satisfies

$$d\psi_t = ((g_t - r)e^{-rt}L_t + re^{-rt}K)dt, \; t \in [0,T]. \tag{1.5.21}$$

Condition (1.5.19) implies that the process ψ is nonincreasing (P-a.s.). The optimality of immediate exercise follows since any waiting strategy leads to a decrease in the discounted payoff.

References

[1] Ait-Sahlia, F. [1995] *Optimal Stopping and Weak Convergence Methods for some Problems in Financial Economics*, Ph.D. Dissertation, Stanford University.

[2] Amin, K. and Khanna, A. [1994] *Convergence of American Option Values from Discrete- to Continuous-Time Financial Models* Mathematical Finance **4**, 289–304.

[3] Bachelier, L. [1900] *Théorie de la Spéculation*. Annales de l'École Normale Supérieure **17**, 21–86; in *The Random Character of Stock Market Prices (Paul H. Cottner, ed.)*, The MIT Press, Cambridge, Mass., 1964.

[4] Barles, G., Burdeau, J., Romano, M. and Samsaen, N. [1995] *Critical Stock Price Near Expiration* Mathematical Finance **5**, 77–95.

[5] Bensoussan, A. [1984] *On the Theory of Option Pricing* Acta Applicandae Mathematicae **2**, 139–158.

[6] Black, F. and Scholes, M. [1973] *The Pricing of Options and Corporate Liabilities* Journal of Political Economy **81**, 637–659.

[7] Boyle, P. P. and Turnbull, S. M. [1989] *Pricing and Hedging Capped Options* Journal of Futures Markets **9**, 41–54.

[8] Brennan, M. and Schwartz, E. [1977] *The Valuation of American Put Options* Journal of Finance **32**, 449–462.

[9] Brennan, M. and Schwartz, E. [1978] *Finite Difference Methods and Jump Processes Arising in the Pricing of Contingent Claims: A Synthesis* Journal of Financial and Quantitative Analysis **13**, 461–474.

[10] Broadie, M. and Detemple, J. B. [1995] *American Capped Call Options on Dividend-Paying Assets* The Review of Financial Studies **8**, 161–191.

[11] Broadie, M. and Detemple, J. B. [1994] *American Option Valuation: New Bounds, Approximations, and a Comparison of Existing Methods* The Review of Financial Studies **9**, 1211-1250.

[12] Broadie, M. and Detemple, J. B. [1994] *The Valuation of American Options on Multiple Assets* Mathematical Finance **7**, 241–286.

[13] Carr, P. and Jarrow, R. [1990] *The Stop-Loss Start-Gain Paradox and Option Valuation: A New Decomposition into Intrinsic and Time Value* The Review of Financial Studies **3**, 469–492.

[14] Carr, P., Jarrow, R. and Myneni, R. [1992] *Alternative Characterizations of American Put Options* Mathematical Finance **2**, 87–106.

[15] Chesney, M., Elliott, R. J. and Gibson, R. [1993] *Analytical Solutions for the Pricing of American Bond and Yield Options* Mathematical Finance **3**, 277–294.

[16] Cox, J. and Ross, S. [1976] *The Valuation of Options for Alternative Stochastic Processes* Journal of Financial Economics **3**, 145–166.

[17] Cox, J. C., Ross, S. A. and Rubinstein, M. [1979] *Option Pricing: A Simplified Approach* Journal of Financial Economics **7**, 229–263.

[18] Cox, J. and Rubinstein, M. [1985] *Option Markets*, Prentice Hall, Englewood Cliffs, New Jersey.

[19] Duffie, D. [1986] *Stochastic Equilibria: Existence, Spanning Number and the 'No Expected Gains from Trade' Hypothesis* Econometrica **54**, 1161–1183.

[20] Duffie, D. [1988] *An Extension of the Black-Scholes Model of Security Valuation* Journal of Economic Theory **46**, 194–204.

[21] El Karoui, N. [1981] *Les Aspects Probabilistes du Controle Stochastique*, Lecture Notes in Mathematics **876**, Springer-Verlag, Berlin, pp. 73–238.

[22] El Karoui, N. and Karatzas, I. [1991] *A New Approach to the Skorohod Problem and its Applications* Stochastics and Stochastics Reports **34**, 57–82.

[23] Flesaker, B. [1992] *The Design and Valuation of Capped Stock Index Options*, Working Paper, University of Illinois at Urbana-Champaign.

[24] Geske, R. [1979] *A Note on an Analytical Valuation Formula for Unprotected American Options on Stocks with Known Dividends* Journal of Financial Economics **7**, 375–380.

[25] Grabbe, O. [1983] *The Pricing of Call and Put Options on Foreign Exchange* Journal of International Money and Finance **2**, 239–253.

[26] Grundy, B. and Wiener, Z. [1995] *Theory of Rational Option Pricing: II*, Working Paper, Wharton School, University of Pennsylvania.

[27] Harrison, M. and Kreps, D. [1979] *Martingales and Arbitrage in Multiperiod Security Markets* Journal of Economic Theory **20**, 381–408.

[28] Harrison, M. and Pliska, S. [1981] *Martingales and Stochastic Integrals in the Theory of Continuous Trading* Stochastic Processes and their Applications **11**, 215–260.

[29] Hull, J. [1997] *Options, Futures, and other Derivative Securities*, Third edition, Prentice Hall, Upper Saddle River, New Jersey.

[30] Jacka, S. D. [1991] *Optimal Stopping and the American Put* Mathematical Finance **1**, 1–14.

[31] Jaillet, P., Lamberton, D. and Lapeyre, B. [1990] *Variational Inequalities and the Pricing of American Options* Acta Applicandae Mathematicae **21**, 263–289.

[32] Karatzas, I. [1988] *On the Pricing of American Options* Applied Mathematics and Optimization **17**, 37–60.

[33] Karatzas, I. and Shreve, S. [1988] *Brownian Motion and Stochastic Calculus*, Springer Verlag, New York.

[34] Kim, I. J. [1990] *The Analytic Valuation of American Options* The Review of Financial Studies **3**, 547–572.

[35] McDonald, R. and Schroder, M. [1998] *A Parity Result for American Options* Journal of Computational Finance **1**, 5-13.

[36] McKean, H. P. [1965] *A Free Boundary Problem for the Heat Equation Arising from a Problem in Mathematical Economics* Industrial Management Review **6**, 32–39.

[37] Merton, R. [1973] *Theory of Rational Option Pricing* Bell Journal of Economics and Management Science **4**, 141–183.

[38] Myneni, R. [1992] *The Pricing of American Options* The Annals of Applied Probability **2**, 1–23.

[39] Roll, R. [1977] *An Analytic Valuation Formula for Unprotected American Call Options on Stocks with Known Dividends* Journal of Financial Economics **5**, 251–258.

[40] Rubinstein M. and Reiner, E. [1991] *Breaking Down the Barriers* Risk **4**, 28–35.

[41] Rutkowski, M. [1994] *The Early Exercise Premium Representation of Foreign Market American Options* Mathematical Finance **4**, 313–325.

[42] Samuelson, P. A. [1965] *Rational Theory of Warrant Pricing* Industrial Management Review **6**, 13–31.

[43] Schwartz, E. S. [1977] *The Valuation of Warrants: Implementing a New Approach* Journal of Financial Economics **4**, 79–93.

[44] van Moerbeke, P. L. [1976] *On Optimal Stopping and Free Boundary Problems* Arch. Rational Mech. Anal. **60**, 101–148.

[45] Whaley, R. E. [1981] *On the Valuation of American Call Options on Stocks with Known Dividends* Journal of Financial Economics **9**, 207–211.

Fields Institute Communications
Volume **22**, 1999

Intergenerational Choice: A Paradox and A Solution

Yuliy Baryshnikov

Department of Mathematics
University of Osnabrück
49069 Osnabrück, Germany
`yuliy@mathematik.uni-osnabrueck.de`

Graciela Chichilnisky

UNESCO Professor Mathematics and Economics
Professor of Statistics
Columbia University
405 Low Library, 116th and Broadway
New York, NY, USA
`gc9@columbia.edu`

Abstract. In the quest for balanced criterion for the problem of intergenerational choice we explore the role played by different groups of generations, which are represented by the Cech-Stone compactification of the naturals.

1 Introduction

In a recent paper Chichilnisky proposed two axioms that capture the idea of sustainable development [**5**]. The axioms require that neither the present nor the future should play a dictatorial role. From the axioms she derived a distinctive welfare criterion that leads to a new form of cost-benefit analysis. These results are summarized in the Appendix.

Here we ask whether these results can be extended to ensure equal treatment not just in the present and the future, but also other groups across time. For example, we may require equal treatment of people who live in even or in odd years, or people who are descendants of two different ethnic groups. We formalize the problem by studying orderings of associated ultrafilters of the integers, where each filter represents a group.

We show that it is generally impossible to find a criterion that ensure equal treatment to all such groups. However in some cases, where the groups are of limited diversity, the earlier results can be extended. In particular when we restrict the groups so that they evolve consistently through time, as shown in Section 5.

We take the set of events to be a countable set, identifying it with the set of naturals **N**.[1] The interpretation of this set is the following: we assume that

---

1991 *Mathematics Subject Classification.* 00A69, 90Axx, 90A80.

[1]In this paper, the setup of Chichilnisky [**5**] is assumed, for details see the Appendix.

it encompasses the totality of instants at which some evaluation of utility is to be exercised. A common situation where such an approach is meaningful is the classical intergenerational distribution. One interprets then the events as generations, and associates to each generation the quality of life, measured in some common units, or the amount of consumption of a certain good shared over generations. We emphasize that the events of utility evaluation are not necessarily time ordered, nor are they bound to happen. Rather, the events enumerate all possible instances at which the mentioned evaluation can happen in principle. Thus, the set can include not just the quality of life for a generation born in, say, year 1990, but *several measurements of qualities* contingent on probable scenarios of development, e.g., on whether or not of effective alternative energy production technologies in 20 years, on climate changes and such. The necessity to compare the qualities for such events is the subtlety often neglected in research on intergenerational choice, but it is clear that a responsible policy formulation should take into account different circumstances which the future generations are to face.

The purpose of this note is to examine the validity of the *evaluation procedures* used in analysis of the socio-economic development. As was shown in [5], many commonly used approaches are giving too much weight to some aspects of the development, neglecting others. Here we try to analyze to what extent one could attempt to refine the evaluation procedure by imposing conditions that the events contingent to some conditions are not neglected. We establish first an impossibility result that one cannot account for *all* possible threads (exact definition below), but has to restrict them somehow. A suggestion on how effectively to produce this restriction concludes the paper.

Our assumption, that the set of events is countable, is a simplification assumed just to present clearly the difficulties already arising in this simple case. We assume no additional structure on $\mathbf{N}$.

2 Notation

The background for the notation and the results of this paper is included in the Appendix, Section 7 below. Denote by $X = C_b(\mathbf{N}) = l^\infty(\mathbf{N})$ the space of feasible utilities streams, that is bounded mappings from $\mathbf{N} \to \mathbf{R}$. Let $\beta\mathbf{N}$ be the Stone-Cech compactification of $\mathbf{N}$; $\beta\mathbf{N}$ coincides as a set with the set of all ultrafilters on $\mathbf{N}$ and the ring of continuous functions on X coincides with the ring of bounded functions on $\mathbf{N}$. In other words, *any* bounded sequence indexed by elements of $\mathbf{N}$ defines a continuous function on $\beta\mathbf{N}$ and vice versa [8].

The space X can be given naturally the structure of Banach space with the *sup* norm on the sequences $\{u_i\} \in X$. Let now $\succ_R$ be a binary preference relation on the space of utility streams X. We assume that the relation $\succ_R$ is given by a Frechet-differentiable function $u : X \to \mathbf{R}$ defined on the Banach space of the bounded functions on $\mathbf{N}$, or, equivalently, the space $C(\beta\mathbf{N})$ (each continuous function on the compact set $C(\beta\mathbf{N})$ is bounded automatically). We will assume that the derivative is continuous in the strong topology (as a mapping from $X \to X^*, x \mapsto u'_x$), with strong (operator) norm on X^* [7]. The relation $\succ_R$ encodes the social preferences over the possible distribution of utilities in the very long run, which take into consideration the situations contingent to some exogenous events. The properties of $\succ_R$ are our main concern. This preference relation should exhibit the intergenerational balance for which we take as a basis the axioms of sustainability as in [5].

Let $x \in X$ and let l_x be the Frechet differential of u at x. By definition, l_x is an element of the dual space to X, that is a continuous linear functional on X. By Riesz' representation theorem, the element corresponds to a (unambiguously defined) Borel measure of finite variation μ_x on βN so that

$$l_x(f) = \int_{\beta N} f d\mu_x.$$

We call this the measure μ_x *associated to* $\succ_R$ *at* x, or simply *associated* when the context makes it unambiguous.

3 Preference relation and measures on βN

In what follows we restrict our attention to the derivatives of the function u defining the preference relations $\succ_R$. This simplification will allow us to concentrate on the features related to the infinite dimensionality of the problem.

First we reformulate the axioms of sustainability [5] to conform to the language of measures on βN.

Sensitivity. *A preference relation* $\succ_R$ *is said to be (strongly) sensitive (at x) if the differential of u at x is strongly positive, that is if $\xi_i' > \xi_i$ for some $i \in N$ and $\xi_j' \geq \xi_j$ for all j, then $l_x(\xi') > (\xi)$.*

The meaning of the strong sensitivity is that an infinitesimally small increment of the utility of a generation yields the increment of the function defining the preference relation *of the same order*.

Sensitivity of the relation $\succ_R$ implies the following property of the associated measure μ_x:

Lemma 3.1 *A preference relation* $\succ_R$ *is sensitive at x if and only if the associated measure gives positive weight to any point of N: $\mu_x(i) > 0$ for any $i \in N$.*

Proof: Obvious. □

Let us consider the (undesirable) properties of the preference relation which are reflected in the dominance of this or that part of the space βN with respect to the measure associated to this preference relation.

Dictatorship of the present. *A preference relation is said to be a dictatorship of the present if any preference $x' \succ_R x$ persists upon 'remote enough' bounded changes of the utility streams x' and x. That is, for any B there exists K such that for any pair $x' \succ_R x$, one has $(x + y) \succ_R (x' + y')$, where y, y' are arbitrary of norm at most 1 and with vanishing first K components.*

In terms of the associated measure, the dictatorship of the present is given as follows:

Lemma 3.2 *A preference relation* $\succ_R$ *is a dictatorship of the present if and only if the associated measure of the growth $N^* = \beta N - N$ is zero at any point of X.*

Proof Denote by L_K the closed subspace of X of elements of $C(N)$ with vanishing first K components. The condition of dictatorship of the present implies that for some $D > 0$ and for any positive $c/2$ there exists number K such that $|u(x + y) - u(x)| \leq c \cdot D/2$ for all $y \in L_K$ and of norm at most D. By assumption, the function u has continuous derivative u'. It follows that for any positive $c/2$, one can find a ball of radius Δ centered at x such that the remainder in the Taylor formula of first order is at most $c/2$ times the norm of perturbation. Combining this all together, one gets (reducing, if necessary, D and Δ so that $D = \Delta$), that

$$|u'_x(\Delta \cdot y)| \leq c \cdot \Delta,$$

or $|l_x(y)| \leq c$ for all $y \in L_K, |y| \leq 1$. In particular, this is valid for the 'departing train' sequence $y_k = (0, \dots, 0, 1, 1, 1, \dots)$ with first nonzero element at k-th place ($k \geq K$). The restriction of the function to the growth $\mathbf{N}^*$ is constant 1 and therefore, $l_x(y_k)$ converges to $\mu_x(\mathbf{N}^*)$. As the μ_x-content of the growth $\mathbf{N}^*$ is at most c with c arbitrary, we get that it vanishes.

The other direction implication is easier: if $\mu_x(y) \leq c$ for all x and all $y \in L_K, |y| \leq 1$, then the norm of $u(x+y) - u(x) = \int_0^1 u'_{x+ty}(y)dt$ can be estimated by c, yielding the desired. $\qquad\square$

Another concept introduced in [5] was that of

Dictatorship of the future. *A preference relation is said to be a dictatorship of the future if any preference $x' \succ_R x$ persists for any finite change of the utility streams x' and x, that is $(x+y) \succ_R (x'+y')$ for any y, y' with only finite number of nonvanishing entries.*

Lemma 3.3 *A preference relation is a dictatorship of the future if and only if the restriction of the associated measure μ_x to the finite part $\mathbf{N} \subset \beta\mathbf{N}$ is zero at any point $x \in X$.*

Proof From the definition of the dictatorship of the future it follows that this property implies the constancy of u along the (finite-dimensional) linear subspaces of X spanned by the vectors with all but a finite number of nonzero components. This is equivalent to the vanishing of all derivatives of u with respect to coordinate vectors of X, that is to vanishing of l_x on all vectors $e_K, K \in \mathbf{N}$, or, equivalently, to $\mu_x(\{K\}) = 0$ for any $K \in \mathbf{N}$. The Lemma follows now from the countability of $\mathbf{N} \subset \beta\mathbf{N}$. $\qquad\square$

Corollary 3.4 *A sensitive relation is not a dictatorship of the future.*

Proof Obvious. $\qquad\square$

One can decompose any measure μ_x into its 'present' and 'future' parts:

$$\mu_x = \mu_x^P + \mu_x^F;$$

with $\mu_x^P = \mu_x \cdot \mathbf{1}_\mathbf{N}; \mu_x^F = \mu_x \cdot \mathbf{1}_{\mathbf{N}^*}$. The Axioms 1 and 2 (no dictatorship to present and no dictatorship to the future) read now as nontriviality of both measures μ_x^P and μ_x^F, see Theorem 7.7. in the Appendix and in [5].

A number of results can be formulated in terms of the interplay between the proper and improper parts of the measure μ_x, describing in particular quite different behavior of the solutions of the optimization problems on different sets of feasible utility streams when the improper part μ_x^F is dropped. We discuss this topic elsewhere.

4 Nondictatorship and threads

This section considers the non-dictatorship assumptions in more detail.

The decomposition result above states that a dictatorship of the future (present) assigns full weight to the corresponding part of $\beta\mathbf{N}$, while non-dictatorial preferences generate *mixed* measures. This conforms well with intuition.

The next step is to distinguish between different parts of the future. Let us return to the compact topological space $\beta\mathbf{N}$. The non-dictatorship conditions reformulated above are just conditions on a measure to assign positive values to both large open sets $\mathbf{N}$ and $\mathbf{N}^*$ (the latter is closed-open in $\beta\mathbf{N}$, to be precise). This ensures that the preference relation "feels" the variations of the compared utility streams.

However, these conditions alone are too rough to reflect precisely the idea of an informed preference relation accounting for possible scenarios of development. Suppose we have a further decomposition of $\beta\mathbf{N}$ into smaller (closed-open) sets. If these sets can be given a meaningful interpretation, so that the collection of the points in any of the sets can be reasonable treated in socio-economic terms, it would be reasonable to expect the associated measures of an informed preference relation to assign positive measures to these sets, that is to take into consideration the utilities for generations exposed to the events constituting the set. Let us illustrate this by an example.

Example Let $\mathbf{N}$ be interpreted just as an infinite sequence of generations, as in the standard setup of the intergenerational choice. Consider the following linear function u as defining the preference relation: if $x = (x_1, x_2, \ldots, x_n, \ldots)$, then

$$u(x) = \sum_{i \geq 1} a_i x_i + \lim{}_B x_{2i},$$

where $a_i > 0$; $\sum_i a_i < \infty$ and $\lim_B$ is a Banach limit [7] taken *over even indices only*. The preference relation defined by u is both future and present dictatorship free, but it exhibits the following pathology: the term responding for the evaluation of the utility streams in the very long run, *ignores completely the asymptotic behavior of the utilities over the generations with odd numbers*.

If one is troubled with such an abstract example, one can think of it in the following terms: consider a major event which influences radically the development (like the hitting of the Earth by a meteorite with mass of several hundred thousand tons, not an impossible event) and number by $2i - 1$ the generation born in year i given the catastrophe, and by $2i$ the generation of year i given no catastrophe. The functional above neglects completely the utility of the generations which happen to live if the catastrophe occurs. This preference relation, while certainly taking into account both present and future, cannot be deemed really responsible!

Of course, one can choose instead of the subset of even numbers any infinite subset of $\mathbf{N}$ such that its complement is infinite as well. One can define again the dictatorship of the present and of the future *for this particular part of* $\mathbf{N}$. It is easy to see that the dictatorships over the whole $\mathbf{N}$ and over S are logically independent if $\mathbf{N} - S$ is infinite. That means that any combination of dictatorships on S and $\mathbf{N} - S$ is possible, for example future dictatorship on S and present dictatorship on $\mathbf{N} - S$.

More formally these properties can be defined as follows:

S-dictatorship. Let S be an infinite subset of $\mathbf{N}$ whose complement in $\mathbf{N}$ is infinite. Such subsets we will call *threads*. The closure of S in $\beta\mathbf{N}$ will be denoted as βS. We will say that a preference relation $\succ_R$ is S-dictatorship of the future at x, if the associated measure μ_l of S is zero, and that it is a S-dictatorship of the present if the associated measure of the growth $S^* = \beta S - S$ is zero. Notice that both of the sets S and S^* are open (and the latter is also closed) in the topology of the Cech-Stone compactification $\beta\mathbf{N}$.

5 A paradox

Now we examine the following problem: how diverse can be threads S be in which the non-dictatorship of the future or the present can be postulated? Modern political correctness suggests that we ought to consider *any* thread (i.e., infinite, coinfinite subset $S \subset \mathbf{N}$). Indeed, if a thread is omitted from consideration, it would mean that this thread is overlooked and that the individuals or generations contingent to events defined by the thread S form a discriminated group whose utilities allocation will be governed by a preference relation neglecting precisely this group. In particular, either of the dictatorships (in their S-restricted formulation) can persist on this thread.

Therefore we will call a preference relation *ideal* if it attaches a positive measure to S and to S^* for any thread S (that is, there is no S-dictatorship of the present or of the future for *any* thread S).

This is a highly desirable property. However, a difficulty arises:

Proposition 5.1 *There exists no ideal preference relation.*

Proof We build on the following fact: there exists a family of infinite coinfinite subsets S_α in $\mathbf{N}$ each two of which have just a finite intersection, which has the cardinality of continuum. A possible construction of this family is the following: identify the set $\mathbf{N}$ with the subset of rational numbers of the unit segment and choose for any number from the segment a sequence of rationals converging to it. These sequences form the family with the required properties.

The growth of the subsets from this family are open-closed subsets in $\beta\mathbf{N}$ and they do not intersect. Therefore, there exists no Borel measure assigning positive values to each of the growths. An ideal preference relation would do exactly this, as the non-dictatorship of the future implies that $\mu_x(S_\alpha^*)$ is positive for all α. Therefore it cannot exist. $\square$

This impossibility result eliminates the hope to construct an ideal preference relation on the utilities streams. One must restrict the totality of threads S where non-dictatorship is required.

6 A solution

The failure to construct an ideal rule stems from the fact that we are trying to consider all ultrafilters, and there are too many of them. The proliferation of ultrafilters can be attributed, roughly, to two circumstances.

Firstly, there are ultrafilters which are in the closures of the threads encompassing entirely unrelated events. For example, one might distinguish a thread consisting of events at all years whose numbers (AD) are prime numbers regardless of the environmental/economic situation; certainly hardly a meaningful thread (exept, perhaps, in some kabbalist tradition).

Secondly, even given a meaningful thread, its compactification contains too many points (more precisely, as many as the whole $\beta\mathbf{N}$). If the thread describes well the development of civilization, a further refinement could be an unnecessary complication.

Therefore, a reasonable strategy to remedy the paradox of the previous section would be: (a) to restrict the variety of threads under consideration, and (b) to identify the ultrafilters in the closure of each given thread. To keep the significant features of the development accounted for, one needs, still, to have a quite involved

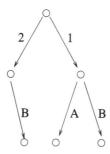

Figure 1 A caricature development tree

structure describing the possible scenarios of the development. It seems reasonable to assume that at each instant, there is just a finite number of significant circumstances influencing the utility at this instant and the course of future development. A formalization of this idea leads to the following definitions.

Recall that we identified the set of events with $\mathbf{N}$. Now we interpret the 'events' in the extended sense, as the set of *histories leading to the events*, e.g., we consider as different the events of exhaustion in 2067 of the mineral oil resources preceded or not by the mastering of effective technologies of sun energy gaining. The set of events *with their prehistories* is again just countable, so the formalism assumed from the beginning is valid unaltered.

Now we have, however, more structure on the set of events than the time order. The events with prehistory can be provided with a *precedence order*.

Definition 6.1 *A precedence order on* $\mathbf{N}$ *is a partial order such that any interval is a finite completely ordered set.*

The intuition behind this definition is that if i precedes j then there exists a *linear* chain of events connecting i to j. In other words, *for each (hypothetical) event i there exists a unique history leading to it*, just as we assumed. A convenient way to think of such an order is to associate a tree to it (recall that a tree is a graph without cycles). One joins two nodes (elements of $\mathbf{N}$) by an edge when one of the events immediately precedes the other (with no further points between them). We orient the edges *from* the preceding nodes (so that the directed paths in the tree correspond to future scenarios. The reverse orientation would give prehistories).

Example A caricature model of the development: in year 1, one invents a protection shield against A Huge Meteorite Hit (case 1) or not (case 2). In year 2, one has therefore two events (contingent on which of the cases realizes). Further, in year 2 a Huge Meteorite Hit happens (case A) or not (case B). In year 3 one has therefore three events, contingent on cases 1A, 1B and 2A. The corresponding tree is shown on Figure 1.

An event can give rise to several different developments; that means that one has to distinguish between the events which happen in different scenarios of the development. A model of evaluation of future development which does not distinguish between ancestors living with or without energy shortage or with or without forest devastation is hardly well fitted.

In general, possible developments form an infinite tree. The trees we consider are provided also with height function. Recall that height function is an integer-valued function on the vertices of the tree such that its values at the neighboring vertices differ by one. In our case, the time (instant of the event) plays the role of the height function. A path in a tree is descending if the height function monotonously increases along it. Two events (vertices of the tree) are joined by a descending path if and only if one of them affects the other. For a linear history case the tree is just a line.

It is worth recalling that an infinite tree which has all nodes of finite degree, has infinite length, that is it possesses an infinite oriented path (which can be unique).

For a point i, we will call all points to which i precedes, the *consequences of i* and denoted by $C(i) \subset \mathbf{N}$. Now we are ready to define our revised non-dictatorship conditions.

Definition 6.2 *A preference relation $\succ_R$ is said be neglecting consequences of i (at x) if the growth of $C(i)$ in $\beta\mathbf{N}$ (that is $\overline{C(i)} - C(i)$) has zero measure with respect to μ_x.*

For a linearly developing history, the neglect of consequences of any i is equivalent to the dictatorship of the present. It is immediate that the dictatorship of the present implies neglecting of consequences of *any* point i.

Proposition 6.3 *For any precedence order of infinite length such that the degree of each point is at most countable, there exist preference relations giving no dictatorship role to the future and not neglecting consequences of any generation i.*

Proof We just sketch the construction. Given the tree with at most countable degree of each point, one can construct a subtree having no finite leaves (that is, any oriented path there can be infinitely extended). For any vertice in this subtree one attaches positive weigths summing up to 1 to its out-edges. Set the measure of $C(i)^*$ (i.e., the growth of the set of consequences of i) to be the product of weights of the edges of the (unique) path from the root to i. This defines a (probability) measure on the σ-algebra generated by growths of $C(i)$'s assigning positive weight to each of them. Extending this measure to the Borel algebra in an arbitrary way gives the desired infinite part. Adding an appropriate finite part of the measure concludes the construction.   □

A more sophisticated view of the construction above is the following: we actually *restrict the freedom of choice of threads*: no thread with causally disconnected instants are allowed now. What is more, we do not distinguish between 'interlaced' threads, that is subsets of the same infinite descending chain in the tree. Topologically, this means that first one reduces $\beta\mathbf{N}$ to a smaller set (the closure of subset corresponding to infinite descending chains) and, secondly, factorizes the resulting (still very large) compact by the 'interlacing' relation. What results is a totally disconnected Hausdorff compact with countable base (modeled by the Cantor continuum), which can be provided with a measure having reasonable properties. In more advanced terms, the resulting space is *the space of ends of the causal tree.*

Remark The naive redefinition of the non-dictatorship of the present along any descending path in the development tree, requiring a positive measure to the closure of the vertices of the path in $\beta\mathbf{N}$, is impossible: there exists continuum of paths again.

7 Appendix (by G. Chichilnisky)

See also [5]. Consider an infinitely lived world, an assumption that obviates the need to make decisions contingent on an unknown terminal date. Each generation is represented by an integer $g, g = 1...\infty$. Generations could overlap or not; indeed one can in principle consider a world in which some agents are infinitely long lived. In this latter case, one is concerned about the manner in which infinitely long lived agents may wish to inject considerations of sustainability into the evaluation of development paths for their own futures.

In order to compare the axioms and results to those of optimal growth theory, I shall adopt a formulation which is as close as possible to that of the neoclassical model. Each generation g has a utility function u_g for consumption of n goods, some of which could be environmental goods such as water, or soil, so that consumption vectors are in R^n, and $u_g : R^n \to R$. The availability of goods in the economy could be constrained in a number of ways, for example by a differential equation which represents the growth of the stock of a renewable resource[2], and/or the accumulation and depreciation of capital. Ignore for the moment population growth; this issue can be incorporated at little change in the results[3]. The space of all feasible consumption paths is indicated $F.:1$

$$F = \{x : x = \{x_g\}_{g=1,2...}, \ x_g \in R^n\}. \tag{7.1}$$

In common with the neoclassical growth literature, utility across generations is assumed to be comparable. Each generation's utility functions are bounded below and above and we assume $u_g : R^n \to R^+$, and $\sup_{x \in R^n} (u_g(x)) < \infty$. This is not a restrictive assumption: one cannot have utilitities which grow indefinitely in either the positive or the negative direction when there are an infinite number of generations[4]. In order to eliminate some of the most obvious problems of comparability I normalize the utility functions u_g so that they all share a common bound, which I assume without loss to be 1:

$$\sup_g (u_g(x_g))_{x_g \in R^n} \leq 1. \tag{7.2}$$

The space of *feasible utility streams* Ω is therefore

$$\Omega = \{\alpha : \alpha = \{\alpha_g\}_{g=1,2...}, \ \alpha_g = u_g(x_g)\}_{g=1,2,...} \text{ and } x = \{x_g\}_{g=1,2...} \subset F\} \tag{7.3}$$

Because I normalized utilities, each utility stream is a sequence of positive real numbers, all of which are bounded by 1. The space of all utility streams is therefore

---

[2]See [3], [2].

[3]Population growth and utilitarian analysis are known to make an explosive mix, which is however outside the scope of this paper.

[4]This would lead to paradoxical behavior. The argument parallels interestingly that given by Arrow [1] on the problem that originally gave rise to Daniel Bernouilli's famous paper on the "St. Petersburg paradox", see *Utility Boundedness Theorem*, page 27. If utilities are not bounded, one can find a utility stream for all generations with as large a welfare value as we wish, and this violates standard continuity axioms.

contained in the space of all bounded sequences of real numbers, denoted ℓ_∞[5]. The welfare criterion W should rank elements of Ω, for all possible $\Omega \subset \ell_\infty$.

7.1 Sensitivity and completeness. The welfare criterion W must be represented by an increasing real valued function on the space of all bounded utility streams[6] $W : \ell_\infty \to R^+$. The word increasing means here that if a utility stream α is obtained from another β by increasing the welfare of some generation, then W must rank α strictly higher than β [7]. This eliminates the Rawlsian criterion and the basic needs criterion, both of which are insensitive to the welfare of all generations but those with the lowest welfare. Completeness and sensitivity eliminate the Ramsey criterion as well as the overtaking criterion.

7.2 The present. How to represent the present? Intuitively, when regarding utility streams across generations, the present is the part of those streams that pertains to finitely many generations. The present will therefore be represented by all the parts of feasible utility streams which have no future: for any given utility stream α, its "present" is represented by all finite utility streams which are obtained by cutting α off after any number of generations. Formally,

Definition 7.1 *For any utility stream $\alpha \in \ell_\infty$, and any integer K, let α^K be the "$K-cutoff$" of the sequence α, the sequence whose coordinates up to and including the $K - th$ are equal to those of α, and zero after the $K - th$.[8]*

Definition 7.2 *The present consists of all feasible utility streams which have no future, i.e., it consists of the cutoffs of all utility streams.*

7.3 No dictatorial role for the present.

Definition 7.3 *We shall say that a welfare function $W : \ell_\infty \to R$ gives a dictatorial role to the present, or that W is a dictatorship of the present, if W is insensitive to the utility levels of all but a finite number of generations, i.e., W is only sensitive to the "cutoffs" of utility streams, and it disregards the utility levels of all generations from some generation on.*

Definition 7.4 *The "K-th tail" of a stream $\alpha \in \ell_\infty$, denoted α_K, is the sequence with all coordinates equal to zero up to and including the K-th, and with coordinates equal to those of α after the K-th[9].*

Formally: for every two utility streams $\alpha, \gamma \in \ell_\infty$ let (α^K, γ_K) be the sequence defined by summing up or "pasting together" the K-th cutoff of α with the K-th tail of γ. W is a dictatorship of the present if for any two utility streams α, β
$$W(\alpha) > W(\beta) \Leftrightarrow$$

---

[5]Formally, $\Omega \subset \ell_\infty$,where $\ell_\infty = \{y : y = \{y_g\}_{g=1,\ldots} : y_g \in R^+, \sup_g | y_g | < \infty\}$. Here $| . |$ denotes the absolute value of $y \in R$, which is used to endow ℓ_∞ with a standard Banach space structure, defined by the norm $\|.\|$ in ℓ_∞

$$\|y\| = \sup_{g=1,2\ldots} | y_g | . \tag{7.4}$$

The space of sequences ℓ_∞ was first used in economics by G. Debreu [6].

[6]The representability of the order W by a real valued function can be obtained from more primitive assumptions, such as, e.g., transitivity, completeness and continuity conditions on W.

[7]Formally, if $\alpha > \beta$ than $W(\alpha) > W(\beta)$.

[8]In symbols: $\alpha^K = \{\sigma_g\}_{g=1,2\ldots}$ such that $\sigma_g = \alpha_g$ if $g \leq K$, and $\sigma_g = 0$ if $g > K$.

[9]In symbols: $\sigma_K = \{\sigma_g\}_{g=1,2\ldots}$ such that $\sigma_g = 0$ if $g \leq K$, and $\sigma_g = \alpha_g$ if $g > K$.

$\exists\, N = N(\alpha, \beta)$ s.t. if $K > N$, $W(\alpha^K, \gamma_K) > W(\beta^K, \sigma_K)$ for any utility streams $\gamma, \sigma \in \infty^{10}$.

The following axiom eliminates dictatorships of the present:

- *Axiom 1: No dictatorship of the present.*

This axiom can be seen to eliminate all forms of discounted sums of utilities, as shown in Theorem 1, Chichilnisky[11] [5].

7.4 The Future. For any given utility stream α, its "future" is represented by all infinite utility streams which are obtained as the "tail" resulting from modifying α to assign zero utility to any initial finite number of generations.

7.5 No dictatorial role for the future.

Definition 7.5 *Welfare function $W : \ell_\infty \to R$ gives a dictatorial role to the future, or equivalently W is a dictatorship of the future, if W is insensitive to the utility levels of any finite number of generations, or equivalently it is only sensitive to the utility levels of the "tails" of utility streams.*

Formally, for every two utility streams α, β

$$W(\alpha) > W(\beta) \Leftrightarrow$$
$$\exists\, N = N(\alpha, \beta) \text{ s.t. if } K > N, \ W(\gamma^K, \alpha_K) > W(\sigma^K, \beta_K) \ \forall \ \gamma, \sigma \ \in \ell_\infty.$$

The welfare criterion W is therefore only sensitive to the utilities of "tails" of streams, and in this sense the future always dictates the outcome independently of the present. The following axiom eliminates dictatorships of the future:

- *Axiom 2: No dictatorship of the future.*

This axiom excludes all welfare functions which are defined solely as a function of the limiting behavior of the utility streams. For example, it eliminates the lim-inf and the long run average.

Definition 7.6 *A sustainable preference is a complete sensitive preference satisfying Axioms 1 and 2.*

7.6 Existence and characterization of sustainable preferences.

Theorem 7.7 *There exists a sustainable preference $W : \ell_\infty \to R$, i.e., a preference which is sensitive and does not assign a dictatorial role to either the present or the future:*

$$W(\alpha) = \sum_{g=1}^{\infty} \lambda_g \alpha_g + \phi(\alpha), \tag{7.5}$$

where $\forall g$, $\lambda_g > 0$, $\sum_{g=1}^{\infty} \lambda_g < \infty$, and where $\phi(\alpha)$ is the function $\lim_{g\to\infty}(\alpha_g)$ extended to all of ℓ_∞ via Hahn-Banach theorem.

Proof   See [4].   □

---

[10]Recall that all utility streams are in ℓ_∞ and they are normalized so that $\sup_{g=1,2...}(\alpha(g)) = \|\alpha\| < 1$ and $\sup_{g=1,2...}(\beta(g)) = \|\beta\| < 1$.

[11]Boundedness of the utilities is important here, although as shown above, it is not a strong assumption, see Arrow's [1] Utility Boundedness Theorem.

Theorem 7.8 *Let $W : \ell_\infty \to R^+$ be a continuous independent sustainable preference. Then W is of the form $\forall \alpha \in \ell_\infty$:*

$$W(\alpha) = \sum_{g=1}^{\infty} \lambda_g \alpha_g + \phi(\alpha) \tag{7.6}$$

where $\forall g\ \lambda_g > 0$, $\sum_{g=1}^{\infty} \lambda_g < \infty$, and ϕ is a purely finitely additive measure.

Proof   See [4].   □

References

[1] Arrow, K. [1964], *Aspects of the Theory of Risk-Bearing*, Yrjö Jahnsson Lectures, Yrjo Jahonssonin Säätio, Helsinki.

[2] Beltratti, A., Chichinisky, G. and Heal, G. [1995], *The Green Golden Rule: valuing the long run*, Working Paper, Columbia University, Economic Letters **49**, pp 175-9.

[3] Chichilnisky, G. [1993], *North-South Trade and the Dynamics of Renewable Resources*, in Structural Change and Economic Dynamics, vol 4 No.2, pp. 219-248.

[4] Chichilnisky, G. [1996], *An axiomatic approach to sustainable development*, Soc Choice Welfare **13**, 231-257.

[5] Chichilnisky, G. [1997], *What is Sustainable Development?*, Land Economics, November 1997, 73(4):467-91.

[6] Debreu, G., *Valuation equilibrium and Pareto optimum*, Pro Nat Acad Sciences **40**, 588-592.

[7] Dunford, N. and Schwarz, J., *Linear operators*, 1, Interscience Publ.

[8] Walker, R. [1974], *The Stone-Cech compactification*, Springer.